S0-AVX-015

DISCARDED

VILLAGE BRANCH
The Farmington Library
Farmington, CT 06032

Paradoxes of Fame

Portrait of Francis Scott Key
by Joseph Wood, ca 1814.
Library of Congress.

Paradoxes of Fame

The Francis Scott Key Story

Sam Meyer

VILLAGE BRANCH
The Farmington Library
Farmington, CT 06034

EASTWIND PUBLISHING

Annapolis, Maryland

B
KEY, FRANCIS SCOTT

Published by Eastwind Publishing
Annapolis, Maryland

© 1995 Eastwind Publishing
First Edition

All rights reserved. No part of this book may be used or
reproduced in any manner without the permission of the
publisher except in the case of brief quotations embodied in
critical reviews or articles. For information about permission
to reproduce selections from this book write to the Publisher,
Eastwind, P.O. Box 1773, Annapolis, MD 21404.

Library of Congress Card Number: 95-060983

Meyer, Sam
    Paradoxes of Fame.
    The Francis Scott Key Story

    Includes bibliographical references and index

ISBN 1-88457-06-5

Manufactured in the United States of America

BR

To the memory of Edward S. Delaplaine
(1893-1989)

It is sublime to have so lived that when one's mortal remains have returned to dust, that dust consecrates and hallows the dust to which it has returned and the life leaves an imprint which the ravages of time cannot dull but brighten. Silent though be the tomb, the life still speaketh and Key's memory dwelleth forever, engraven upon that endeared emblem, the flag of our country.

Francis Scott Key-Smith

Contents

List of Illustrations

The Star Spangled Banner

O say, can you see, by the dawn's early light,
    What so proudly we hailed, at the twilight's last gleaming?
Whose broad stripes and bright stars through the perilous fight,
    O'er the ramparts we watched, were so gallantly streaming;
And the rockets' red glare, the bombs bursting in air,
Gave proof through the night that our flag was still there:
O say does that Star Spangled Banner yet wave
O'er the land of the free and the home of the brave?

On that shore, dimly seen through the mists of the deep,
    Where the foe's haughty host in dread silence reposes,
What is that which the breeze, o'er the towering steep,
    As it fitfully blows, now conceals, now discloses?
Now it catches the gleam of the morning's first beam,
In full glory reflected now shines in the stream:
'Tis the Star Spangled Banner; O long may it wave
O'er the land of the free and the home of the brave!

And where are the foes who so vauntingly swore
    That the havoc of war, and the battle's confusion,
A home and a country should leave us no more:
    Their blood has washed out their foul footsteps' pollution;
No refuge could save the hireling and slave
From the terror of flight, or the gloom of the grave;
And the Star Spangled Banner in triumph doth wave
O'er the land of the free and the home of the brave!

O thus be it ever, when freemen shall stand
    Between their loved homes and the war's desolation;
Blest with victory and peace, may the heav'n-rescued land
    Praise the Power that hath made and preserved us a nation!
Then conquer we must, when our cause it is just,
And this be our motto, "In God is our trust;"
And the Star Spangled Banner in triumph shall wave
O'er the land of the free and home of the brave!

from Poems of the Late Francis Scott Key, Esq., 1857

Earliest extant copy in the hand of Francis Scott Key of "The Star-Spangled Banner," ca 15-16 September 1814. Maryland Historical Society, Baltimore, Md.

Acknowledgments

I wish to acknowledge with appreciation the cooperation given to me in the preparation of this study by numerous libraries, historical societies, and other institutions but special mention is owed to the following: Annapolis, Md.: Hall of Archives, State of Maryland. Baltimore, Md.: Enoch Pratt Free Library; Fort McHenry National Monument and Historic Shrine; The Maryland Historical Society. Chicago, Il.: Newberry Library; Regenstein Library, University of Chicago. Frederick, Md.: *Frederick News-Post*; Mt. Olivet Cemetery. San Francisco, Ca.: Public Information Office, City and County of San Francisco. Washington, D.C.: Francis Scott Key Foundation, Inc.; Library of Congress; Martin Luther King Memorial Library; The Historical Society of Wasington, D.C. Upper Marlboro, Md.: Prince Georges's County Historical Society.

For permission to reprint Chapter 7, I thank *Periodical, Journal of the Council on America's Military Past* and likewise thanks to *Maryland Historical Magazine* for consenting to reprinting of Chapter 2.

The dedication to Edward S. Delaplaine is intended as a tribute to the memory of one who throughout his entire adult life, in his numerous writings and addresses, signalized the contributions of Francis Scott Key to his country. I had the pleasure of conversing in person with Mr. Delaplaine on two occasions toward the end of his life: first, at the rededication of the Key monument at Mt.Olivet Cemetery on 7 June 1987, and, second, at the residence in Frederick of himself and his wife, Helen, in November of 1988. Following the publication of my first article on Key in the fall of 1987, Judge Delaplaine, as he was popularly known, having served eighteen years as Associate Justice of Maryland's highest court, the Court of Appeals, welcomed me warmly as a "fellow worker in the vineyard." This was in a note on the flyleaf of his last work, *John Philip Sousa and the National Anthem.*

My warm thanks go to my publisher, D. Patrick Hornberger, who believed in this book. I also wish to acknowledge the help given by Melissa McNitt as editor.

And finally I express my love and gratitude to my dear wife, Sarah, and to our children, Harris, Robin, Lindy, and June for their encouragement (as well as forbearance!) during the years I was engaged on this study of Francis Scott Key.

Sam Meyer
Chicago, Illinois

Preface

In the past half century, scholars have largely rescued Francis Scott Key from the comparative obscurity of being known almost exclusively for composing the words to "The Star-Spangled Banner." I hope this volume will bring Key into a larger perspective by presenting fresh aspects of the roles he played in the first half of the nineteenth century.

As for "The Star-Spangled Banner," its popularity has waxed and waned since it first saw print shortly after the Battle of Baltimore and North Point during the late summer of 1814. In spite of its official designation as the national anthem on 3 March 1931, heated criticism of it and pleas for its replacement by a "more suitable" patriotic song continue to this day, especially around Flag Day and 14 September, the anniversary of the anthem's birth. The arguments employed endlessly repeat those voiced during the years before Congress passed the enabling act: "The Star-Spangled Banner" is too martial; it is hard to memorize and to sing; its tune is that of an English tavern song; and in the third stanza it insults the British.

The theme of fame vis-à-vis "The Star-Spangled Banner" and its creator extends through all the chapters except Chapter 4, which is about Dr. William Beanes. Key and John S. Skinner rescued Dr. Beanes from imprisonment on a ship of His Royal Majesty's Fleet; the rescue occasioned the writing of the national song. In his lifetime, Key enjoyed a most favorable reputation, and not solely because he wrote the popular patriotic hymn. Although modest and self-effacing, his varied talents as a scholar (he was valedictorian of his graduating class at St. John's College in Annapolis, Maryland), lawyer, orator, lay church leader, and civic servant were so outstanding that his light could not be hidden. He was held in high esteem by virtually all who came into contact with him. He was on friendly terms, for example, with such notable contemporaries as Bishop William Meade of Virginia, and national legislators and fellow attorneys like Daniel Webster, Henry Clay, John Calhoun, and William Pinckney. He had a personal relationship with Presidents James Madison, Andrew Jackson, James Monroe, and Martin Van Buren. Yet throughout his life Key remained an essentially private person, whose only really close friend was the eccentric Virginian, John Randolph of Roanoke, a frequent house guest of the Keys during his several congressional terms. Key was extremely devoted to his wife,

Mary, whom he called "Polly," to his children, and to his parents, John Ross and Anne Phoebe Key. On 4 March 1807, seven years before he achieved minor celebrity status as the author of "The Star-Spangled Banner," Key wrote to his parents: "I would rather see you satisfied and hear you say with joy 'this is my son' than receive the applause of the whole world."

This statement suggests the elements of paradox and irony that underlie the Key story. This thread of contrariety runs throughout the book, showing an overlooked richness and complexity of Key's life, his song, and his fame.

One indication of this oversight is that there were no highly visible remembrances of Key in Washington until recently. What appears to be the most obvious memorial to him— the Francis Scott Key Bridge connecting Washington, D.C. and Rosslyn, Virginia— is shown on maps simply as "Key Bridge" and is not associated with his name by tourists or even residents of Washington. Notwithstanding all the statues scattered through the city on the Potomac, not a single one was of Key. Moreover, according to Carlton J. Corliss, a member of the District of Columbia Historical Society, in an unpublished paper of 1948, there was even at that late date no likeness of Frank Key, as he was known to his friends, among the numerous art galleries and museums of the city. Yet Key lived with his family in Washington for nearly forty years. He had practiced law in his adoptive city until his death in 1843, often arguing cases before the Supreme Court of the United States. He had been Attorney General for the Federal District from 1833 to 1841. And he had authored the official anthem of the United States. Chapter 1 contrasts Key's lifelong disavowal of worldly renown with his aspiration to win eternal glory in the Hereafter—to await, as he put it in one of his poems, "the loud hallelujahs of angels" welcoming the soul to its eternal home in the skies. Chapter 2 on Key's religious life, character, and leadership in the church points out how his memory has been perpetuated virtually on the basis of one deed, writing the poem on the starry banner, whereas his outstanding activities in other areas, specially in the sphere of religion, have been forgotten. Yet the ode itself was but one manifestation of his Christian faith and practice, in which religious, patriotic, and literary impulses merged.

Chapter 3 explores the possible contradiction between, on the one hand, the image of Key projected in "The Star-Spangled Banner" as a zealous follower of his government's mandates and as a fighter to preserve a nation where "freemen shall stand" and, on the other, his actual role as a soldier-patriot and as a slaveholder. Chapter 4 on William Beanes relates how a country doctor from Upper Marlboro, a small town in Maryland, came, through the whimsicalities of time and chance, to be the incidental cause of the writing of what was to become the premier song of the nation. In the event, he achieved, with no volition on his part, a modest but secure niche in the annals of his country.

Chapter 5 takes up in full and fresh detail paradoxes that have encompassed Francis Scott Key and "The Star-Spangled Banner" from the beginning. It focuses on topics of ironic implications untreated in previous chapters. These are the unsuccessful bids to get Key's name inscribed on the tablet in the Hall of Fame; the prolonged seesaw struggle in Congress to determine which song among several strong candidates would eventually win the distinction of being designated the official national anthem; and the pros and cons of the continuing charges leveled against the Banner song by its opponents.

Chapter 6 on Key monuments reveals the irony of five sculptured statues—and one installed as recently as 14 September 1993, in the new Francis Scott Key Park in Georgetown of the nation's capital—erected to commemorate the earthly fame of a man, when everything known about him confirms that he would not have wanted them. He would not have desired to be so exalted, firmly believing, as John Milton expressed it in his famous elegy on his friend, Edward King, that "true fame grows not on mortal soil."

Chapter 7 recounts three failed attempts, prior to the completion of the Francis Scott Key Park in 1993, to create in Washington a shrine to the memory of Francis Scott Key. It further describes the earlier remembrances to Key that still exist in the capital.

In the October 1887 issue of *The Magazine of American History*, one Horatio King harkened back more than forty years to his contact with Francis Scott Key toward the end of the latter's life in these words: "I remember him about that time as a mild, agreeable, entertaining gentleman." At the dedication of the monument over Key's grave at Mt. Olivet Cemetery in Frederick, Maryland, on 9 August 1898, Henry Watterson, editor of the Louisville *Courier-Journal*, asserted that Key's life of sixty-three years was "an unbroken idyll of tranquil happiness" and compared his career in its calm serenity with that of the village priest described in Oliver Goldsmith's *The Deserted Village*. Watterson, born in 1840, never of course, knew Key. Nor was he apparently aware that Frank and Polly Key had their full share of human sorrow, not the least of which being the untimely deaths of three of their six sons: Edward, 6, by accidental drowning in the Potomac; Daniel, 23, by receiving a mortal wound in a gun duel with another midshipman; and John, 28, by succumbing to a sudden and unexplained illness.

It is hoped that the Francis Scott Key that emerges from the pages of this thematic and interpretive study will be seen as a many-faceted human much more complex and interesting than was suggested by the remarks of King and Watterson.

The original Star-Spangled Banner that flew over Fort McHenry on 13-14 September 1814. Displayed in the National Museum of American History, The Smithsonian Institution, Washington, D.C.

Chapter 1

Away from the World's Vain Gaze

Many school history books used to include a reproduction of a colorful canvas by Percy Moran painted in 1912 called "By Dawn's Early Light." It depicts a young man standing on the top of a ladder leading to the taffrail of a small boat. With his right hand flung outward, gesturing toward the shore, he is looking rapturously at an enormous flag, seen at a distance waving over the embattled ramparts of Fort McHenry. The fort was the star-shaped bastion that guarded —and still does symbolically—the seaward approaches to Baltimore, the third largest city in the country at the time. The man in the picture is, of course, Francis Scott Key, an attorney from Georgetown barely past his thirty-fifth birthday.

Whether you have seen this painting or not, you are certain to know the sequel to this scene. After the furious twenty-five hour British bombardment of the fort by bomb and rocket "our flag was still there." At daybreak on 14 September 1814, Key dashed off the first part of the song on the back of an old letter. He completed the poem at a hotel when he returned to Baltimore. The poem was first printed and distributed as a handbill and shortly thereafter published in newspapers. It fired the imagination of citizen, soldier, and sailor alike until in 1931 by an Act of Congress and President Herbert Hoover's signature it became the official national anthem of the United States.

Historians of the past half century or more have been busy delving into many unexplored aspects of Francis Scott Key's life and career. He is no longer regarded in the way he apparently was in 1935, when Victor Weybright wrote in the first standard biography of Key: ". . . like most Maryland celebrities he is now a vague figure, his life eclipsed by one spectacular deed."[1] Scholars have since rounded out the picture of Key in the roles of a family man,

"By Dawn's Early Light," 1912 oil on canvas by Edward Percy Moran (1862-1935). Painted for the National Star-Spangled Banner Centennial and Dedication of Fort McHenry as a national park, 12-13 September 1914. Original in the Peale Museum, Baltimore. The Library of Congress.

lawyer, militia officer, poet, orator, churchman, statesman, and civic leader.

Nevertheless, some leading questions concerning Key and the patriotic hymn have been neglected. What, for example, was Key's attitude toward his literary creation? And how did he respond to the recognition that he received because of it?

Details of Key's feelings about the song are sparse, but those that do exist show how, in the face of mounting evidence that it was not destined to be merely a "flash in the pan," like so many other war ballads of the time, he never allowed its success to turn his head.

In the beginning Key truly had no idea that his song would survive. He had been inspired to write it at a moment of high emotion when he glimpsed his country's flag still waving, proof that the fort had withstood the furious onslaught by land and sea. He was always writing down on anything handy his thoughts in meter and rhyme.[2] He never took anything beyond modest satisfaction in any of his poetic efforts. His verses circulated only among his family and intimate friends.[3] A slender collection of his verses was published posthumously, containing traditional obituary, religious, amatory, and mildly humorous pieces.

But the song that the lawyer-poet began composing on the U.S. truce-boat in Baltimore harbor became an instant hit upon its first printing as a handbill on 17 September 1814, followed by publication in the Baltimore *Patriot* on 20 September and the Baltimore *American* on the twenty-first, all without attribution of authorship. By 19 October, the first sheet music issue of the new song was produced by Thomas Carr in Baltimore. Key's name does not appear, but the tune is noted as "Anacreon in Heaven," the title of the English tavern song whose air had been used for dozens of popular ballads in America. The best known of these was "Adams and Liberty" by Robert Treat Paine, Jr., first sung on 4 July 1798, at a fireman's banquet. Key himself had employed the tune in a verse tribute set to music in honor of the naval heroes returning in 1804 from the Barbary Coast war in the Mediterranean.

When the War of 1812 ended, Key's ode declined somewhat in popularity until it again reached a peak during the Civil War. Its authorship, nevertheless, was well known and during the remainder of Key's life the song was frequently sung, played, performed dramatically, and widely reprinted in newspapers, magazines, songbooks, and annuals. On Capitol Hill, orators, referring to him by name, often quoted "the land of the free and the home of the brave." In his travels, bands would often play the song for his benefit, and even strangers were in the habit of beseeching him to autograph their albums.

From the start the song seemed to proceed on its own momentum. Key never had to "puff" it, which he was not inclined to do anyway. He was not the one who hurried the manuscript to the *Patriot* for its initial printing as a flyer on the day after his return to Baltimore, following his detention on the flag-of-truce vessel by the British. It was either Judge Joseph Hopper Nicholson, Key's brother-in-law, who had been second in command at Fort McHenry during the battle, or John S. Skinner, U.S. government agent for the exchange of prisoners and who in his official capacity had accompanied Key on the historic mission to rescue Dr. William Beanes who brought the poem to the newspaper office.[4] The physician from Upper Marlboro, Maryland, had been imprisoned by the British for an alleged breach of faith by helping arrest and jail a few British stragglers who, after the Battle of Bladensburg on 24 August 1814, pillaged their way through Upper Marlboro.

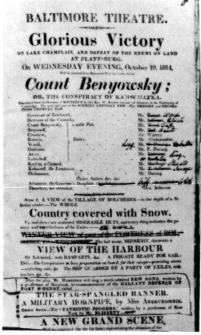

October 18, 1814, theatre advertisement in the Baltimore American *announcing that a "new song written by a gentleman of Maryland" would be sung after the play. Maryland Historical Society, Baltimore.*

The early printing of the anthem had the uninspired caption, "Defence of Fort McHenry," and the earliest known manuscript, in Key's own hand, now preserved in a special marble-lined niche at the Maryland Historical Society in Baltimore, has no title at all.[5] Key was not ascribed authorship until 24 September 1814, when the poem under the "Fort McHenry" title appeared on page three of the *Frederick-Town* [Maryland] *Herald.*[6]

Nor is Key believed to have given the poem its present stirring title. The title first surfaced in a newspaper advertisement in the Baltimore *American* on 18 October 1814, announcing that a Mr. Hardinge would sing "The Star-Spangled Banner" at the Holliday Street Theatre the following day.[7]

It is curious—and significant—that in a long letter of 5 October 1814, to his close friend, John Randolph, Key talks at length about having spent eleven days with the British fleet, about successfully rescuing Dr. Beanes from his English captors, and about Baltimore's miraculous delivery from burning and pillage, but does not mention the song.[8]

In two poetic pieces not intended for publication, Key does allude to his best-known poem. One of these he wrote at the request of Mrs. Sarah Gayle, wife of the Governor of Alabama, for a friend of hers in Tuscaloosa, Alabama. This was in December of 1833 when Key was on a mission to Alabama on behalf of President Andrew Jackson to negotiate an agreement between the federal government and the State of Alabama regarding disputed lands originally ceded to the Creek Indians. In the poem "To Miss—" Key deprecates his own poetic talent. With obvious reference to "The Star-Spangled Banner," he says:

> Not even thy praise can make me vainly deem
> That 'twas the poet's power, and not his theme,
> That woke thy young heart's rapture, when from far
> His song of vict'ry caught thy fav'ring ear:
> That victory was thy country's, and his strain
> Was of that starry banner that again
> Had waved in triumph on the battle plain.[9]

In October of 1840, Key returned to Frederick, Maryland, to visit his blind cousin, Ms. Eleanor Potts, who played some old tunes for him on her guitar. While he was visiting her he wrote a poem. In it he also included a tribute to his mother for the gift of song that she had fostered in him, and he alluded modestly to the repute that his poems—mainly "The Star-Spangled Banner"—had gained for him. The relevant lines are:

> And if the magic power of song
>   Its influence o'er me ever threw,
> And haply some small mead of fame
>   To lay of mine be ever due,
>
> These early teachings at her knee
>   To these, the high-prized boon I owe
> With all the blessings I have known
>   And all I ever hope to know.[10]

In light of the éclat associated with Key as author of "The Star-Spangled Banner" following its debut in 1814, it is all the more remarkable that only once in his life did he publicly refer directly to his authorship of the song. And this acknowledgment came only when taking any other course would have been discourteous to people he admired and respected. He gave this explicit, personal account of how he came to write the ode at a dinner held on the afternoon of 6 August 1834, in the Court Yard of Frederick, not too far from Key's ancestral home of Terra Rubra.[11] The celebration was sponsored by the Jackson Democrats of Frederick County to pay homage to Roger Brooke Taney, who had been Attorney General and Secretary of the Treasury under Jackson and who later succeeded John Marshall as Chief Justice of the Supreme Court of the United States. (Taney was Key's brother-in-law, having married Key's sister, Anne, on 7 January 1806.) Key, now fifty-five, was one of the guests singled out for special recognition. Following Taney's address, a toast was offered to "Francis S. Key—a friend of the administration and an incorruptible patriot; worthy of being honored, wherever genius is admired or liberty cherished, as the author of "The Star-Spangled Banner."

In an eloquent response, Key recalled the events of some twenty years past, speaking of the elation he had felt upon catching a glimpse at daybreak of the Stars and Stripes still flying over the fort:

> You have been pleased to declare your approbation of my song . . . . The song, I know, came from the heart, and if it has made its way to the hearts of men, whose devotion to their country and the great cause of Freedom I know so well, I could not pretend to be insensible to such a compliment.

He concluded on a note of characteristic humility:

> The honor is due, not to me who made the song, but to the heroism of these who made me make it.
>
> I will therefore propose as a toast—The real authors of the song, "The Defenders of *The Star-Spangled Banner*: What they would not strike to a foe, they will never sell to traitors."

The affair at Frederick was the most signal recognition tendered to Key during his lifetime, but Taney, not he, was the guest of honor, and the celebration, was a regional, not a national event.

While he was alive, Key never received the culminating accolades of the kind other composers of famous national songs received. For example, in 1892, the Governor of Massachusetts issued a proclamation that on the four-hundredth anniversary of Columbus' discovery of America—and coincidentally on the eighty-second birthday of Samuel Smith—all the schoolchildren in the state should sing "America" together, in their respective classrooms and auditoriums, to create "one grand chorus."[12] This occasion is similar to one in 1928 when Katherine Lee Bates, who wrote the words to "America the Beautiful," attended the annual Convention of the National Education Association in Minneapolis. At a special session in tribute to her, a chorus of girls representing twenty different nationalities sang her song.[13]

Or what could match the cachet of having a gold medal authorized by Congress presented to you in a televised ceremony by the President of the United States? This happened in 1955 to another composer of patriotic lyrics. On one side of the medal is the inscription: "Presented to Irving Berlin by President Eisenhower in national recognition and appreciation of services in composing many popular songs, including "God Bless America."[14]

If Francis Scott Key had been given such transcendent honors, he undoubtedly would have received them with his customary hu-

Dedication of the Key monument at the Golden Gate Park on the 4th of July, 1888. From Frank Leslie's Illustrated Newspaper, *Library of Congress.*

7

mility. Of strongly Calvinist belief, he aspired neither to fame nor fortune. The many verse epitaphs he wrote for relatives and friends reflect this desire to be "secluded from the world's vain gaze," as he expressed it in an obituary poem of 1826 to the memory of William Hemsley. Hemsley was a former parishioner of St. John's Church, of which Key was a longtime member.[15] The Reverend John T. Brooke, who was well acquainted with Key, having been his pastor in Georgetown for a number of years, emphasized his former congregant's essentially retiring nature in the memorial sermon he delivered at Christ Church, Cincinnati, on 29 January 1843, shortly after Key's death from pneumonia on 11 January.[16]

In 1898, Key would have a dramatic monument dedicated to his memory at his grave site in the Mt. Olivet Cemetery, Frederick, Maryland. Library of Congress.

It is ironic that long after he was laid to rest, elaborate earthly honors, contrary to his deeply held Christian beliefs, were bestowed upon his memory. The most impressive of these attempts to eternalize Key's name came in the form of highly wrought structures of stone and bronze.

The first of many such monuments, a huge edifice of marble and bronze, was erected in Golden Gate Park, San Francisco. Executed in Italy by William W. Story, the monument contained a life-size figure of Key mounted on a travertine pedestal. The dedicatory ceremonies on 4 July 1888, were on a grand scale. Eleven of Key's descendants were present. Two of his grandchildren pulled the cord that uncovered the monument.[17]

On still another national holiday, Flag Day, 14 June 1922, a gigantic statue of the Greek god of Music and Poetry, Orpheus, strumming his lyre, was unveiled on the front lawn of Fort McHenry, now a National Monument and Historic Shrine. The monument was dedicated to the memory of Francis Scott Key and the Defenders of Baltimore in the War of 1812. President Warren G. Harding lent his presence for the occasion to praise the poet-patriot. Among many fine things the President said—and perhaps the most perceptive, in its allusion to Key's freedom from ambition and pretensions to grandeur—was this pronouncement:

> An American citizenship of the high and simple faith of
> Francis Scott Key, aflame for defense, and no less
> devoted in meeting the problems of peace, will add to
> the lustre of the banner he so proudly acclaimed.[18]

Key's own words express most movingly the relationship of the Poet of the Flag to his celebrated lyric. In the speech on the day of jubilee for the Jackson Democrats of Frederick County, Key called up the events of a score of years earlier:

> Through the clouds of war, the stars of that banner still
> shone in my view, and I saw the discomfited host of its
> assailants driven back in ignominy to their ships. Then,
> in that hour of deliverance and joyful triumph, my heart
> spoke; and "Does not such a country, and such defend-
> ers of their country, deserve a song?" was its question.
> With it came an inspiration not to be resisted; and even
> though it had been a hanging matter to make a song, I
> must have written it. Let the praise, then, if any be due,
> be given, not to me, who only did what I could not help
> doing; not the writer, but to the inspirers of the song![19]

Can there be doubt that, like the anthem born in battle, these words too reflected the true spirit of a man to whom "the applause of the whole world," in his own phrase, was distinctly secondary to the glory of the world to come?

Notes

1. Victor Weybright, *Spangled Banner: The Story of Francis Scott Key* (New York: Farrar and Rinehart, Inc., 1935), p. 289.

2. Francis Scott Key-Smith, *Francis Scott Key, Author of The Star-Spangled Banner; What Else He Was and Who* (Washington, D.C.: Key Smith and Co., 1911), p. 80.

3. *Poems of the Late Francis Scott Key, Esq., with an Introductory Letter by Chief Justice Taney*, ed. Henry V.D. Johns (New York: Carter and Bros., 1857), p. vi (hereafter Key, *Poems*).

4. For an extended discussion of the origin and first printing of the poem, later titled "The Star-Spangled Banner," see George J. Svejda, *History of the Star-Spangled Banner from 1814 to the Present* (Washington, D.C.: U.S. Department of the Interior, National Park Service [1969]), pp. 69-83; and P. W. Filby and Edward G. Howard, *Star-Spangled Books* (Baltimore, Md.: Maryland Historical Society, 1972), pp. 41-43.

5. See p. xiii above for photocopy from the original holograph of the earliest surviving manuscript (ca 15 Sept. 1814) of the Banner lyric. All four of the extant copies in Key's handwriting, presented by him as souvenirs to his friends, have minor variations in wording. The earliest was given to Judge Joseph Hopper Nicholson, who commanded an artillery company at the Battle of Baltimore and who was married to the sister of Key's wife. Only one of the surviving copies, a gift to Louis J. Cist in 1840 and now in the Library of Congress, bears a title: "The Star-spangled Banner." For a description of the niche housing the manuscript, see Harold R. and Beta K. Manakee, *The Star-Spangled Banner: The Story of Its Writing by Francis Scott Key at Baltimore, September 13-14, 1814* (Baltimore, Md.: The Maryland Historical Society, 1954), pp. 23-24. For details of the repository arrangements as well as an account of the dedication of the placement of the copy in the Maryland Historical Library and Museum in Baltimore on 14 September 1954, see "The Unveiling of the Original Manuscript of the Star-Spangled Banner, " *Maryland Historical Magazine*, 49, No. 4, Dec. 1954): 255-70.

6. Filby and Howard, pp. 50, 113.

7. Ibid., p. 59.

8. Key to Randolph, 5 Oct. 1814, in Svejda, pp. 66-67.

9. Key, *Poems*, p.45.

10. Ibid., p. 89.

11. For an account of this celebrated dinner, see Edward S. Delaplaine, *Francis Scott Key: Life and Times* (New York: Biography Press, 1937), pp. 374-382, from which passages of Key's speech at Frederick are drawn.

12. C. A. Browne, *The Story of Our National Ballads*, rev. ed. by Willard A. Heaps (New York: Thomas T. Crowell Co., 1960), p. 90. Smith was given an earlier honor most gratifying to him by being included, with eight other distinguished members, in a poem, "The Boys" by Oliver Wendell Holmes, written for the thirtieth Harvard class reunion

in 1859 and published shortly thereafter in a book by Dr. Holmes. The last two lines of the quatrain devoted to Smith read: "But he shouted a song for the brave and the free—/ Just read on his medal, 'My country,' 'of thee!'"

13. Robert Kraske, *America the Beautiful: Stories of Patriotic Songs* (Champaign, Il.: Garrard Publishing Company, 1972), pp. 81-82.

14. Ibid., p. 94.

15. Key, *Poems*, p. 126.

16. John T. Brooke, *A Sketch of the Character of the Late Francis Scott Key* (Cincinnati: Wilson and Drake, 1843), p.8.

17. Raymond E. Clary, historian, to Gomer Pond, Asst. Dean, University of Southern Mississippi, 8 July 1971 (copy furnished to author by Diane Palacio, public information officer, City and County of San Francisco, with cover letter of 18 Sept. 1985).

18. Delaplaine, *Francis Scott Key*, p. 480.

19. Ibid., p. 380.

Chapter 2

Religion, Patriotism, and Poetry

Nearly sixty years ago, a biographer noted that Key was still celebrated "as if he were forever suspended there in history, lute or pen in hand, a man of one exploit whose career before and afterwards is of no consequence."[1] Little has changed since then and paintings like Percy Moran's *By Dawn's Early Light* and the statue of Key at the entrance to Mt. Olivet Cemetery in Frederick, Maryland (where he is buried), reinforce Key's popular image.

The story of the writing of the national anthem has been endlessly repeated, but more than eighty years has passed since Lawrence C. Wroth first explored the theme of Key's deeply religious nature in the *Maryland Historical Magazine*. It is certainly time now to consider this aspect of his life in a larger perspective. For Key, as for many other Americans who grew up in the years following the Revolution, religion and patriotism were virtually fused in their ultimate purpose, as were religion and literature. In an address he delivered late in his life to students at Bristol College in Connecticut, Key stressed the importance of religion in human affairs. There is little point, he contended, in recognizing intellectual achievements while neglecting the "'one thing needful,' the care of the soul"; religion, he declared, "must take high precedence, and hold supreme dominion over every thing belonging to man."[2]

Commentators and political orators rightly refer to "The Star-Spangled Banner" as a hymn; Key intended it to be. Unlike national airs that exalt rulers or like "La Marseillaise" call soldiers to arms, Key's lyric—besides being a paean of praise—was a prayer of thanksgiving to God for having saved the city of Baltimore from the damage the British had wreaked on Washington only three weeks earlier. Francis Scott Key-Smith[3] argued that his great-grandfather's verse breathed a pure, religious sentiment. Writing in 1930, Key-

Smith asserted that the Christian spirit and fortitude of the author manifested itself in the often-forgotten last stanza:

O! thus be it ever, when freemen shall stand
Between their loved home and the war's desolation;
Blessed with vict'ry and peace, may the heav'n rescued
  land
Praise the Power that hath made and preserved us a
  nation!
Then conquer we must, when our cause it is just,
And this be our motto, "In God is our trust!"
And the Star-Spangled Banner in triumph shall wave
O'er the land of the free and the home of the brave![4]

Key first spoke publicly of the tie between religion and patriotism earlier in the year that he witnessed the assault on Fort McHenry. Of medium height, strong and wiry, with brown, wavy hair and dark blue eyes,[5] he was then already known in the courts as a highly effective orator. Invited to address the Washington Society of Alexandria, Virginia, on the founding father's birthday, 22 February, Key stressed Washington's admonition in his farewell address of 1796 that every citizen must adhere to the dictates of religion and morality. He reminded his listeners—many of whom had served with Washington—that the great Virginian had called upon his countrymen to "acknowledge and praise the Power that defended them." "A just and disinterested love of country," Key insisted, "springs from religion as from its natural and proper source, and is ever nourished by its influence."[6]

In 1814 Key was a devout and learned Episcopalian, thoroughly familiar with the English statesman and leader of the Anglican evangelical party, William Wilberforce. Key subscribed fully to Wilberforce's view that the Gospels supplied the only trustworthy guide to Christian conduct. In Wilberforce's *A Practical View of the Prevailing Religious System of Professed Christians* (published in 1787, with twenty-five American reprints by 1826), Key found precedent for his conviction that religious faith and patriotism go hand in hand. For Wilberforce, patriotism was not a domineering quality that prompted men to aggrandize their own country by the oppression and conquest of others; to that "patriotism," he declared, religion—representing justice, peace, and goodwill—must indeed be an enemy. The British lay leader instead defined patriotism as a

quality that bound men and women to their homeland without con-
fining philanthropy to a single nation. "Of this true patriotism,"
wrote Wilberforce, "Christianity is the most copious source and the
surest preservative."[7]

Key's "Hymn for the Fourth of July 1832" highlighted this
link between religious devotion and patriotism. Key implored the
Lord to bestow His blessings on a free and rescued land and closed
with a special prayer for its fallen heroes: "And when in power he
comes, / O, may our native land, / From all its rending tombs, / Send
forth a glorious band!"[8] This patriotic verse appeared in *Poems*,
posthumously published in 1857 and edited by the Reverend Henry
V. D. Johns, who noted that Key's friends had long treasured his
poetry. Johns' book merits attention because it displayed so well
Key's feelings of patriotism and religion. "The Star-Spangled Banner" opened the thin volume. Of the fifty-six selections in *Poems*,
twenty-seven were devotional, suggesting their author's spiritual
character. Six were considered of sufficiently high quality to be
contained in a prestigious collection published in 1868, *Lyra Sacra
Americana*.[9] Here Key was in the company of younger contempo-
raries like Henry Wadsworth Longfellow (four poems); Oliver
Wendell Holmes, whose "Old Ironsides" celebrated the frigate
Constitution's prominent part in the War of 1812 (also four); the
Reverend Samuel F. Smith, whose "America" song rivaled "The Star-
Spangled Banner" as a leading national ode (one); and perhaps the
best hymn writer of them all, the Reverend William Augustus
Muhlenberg of the Protestant Episcopal Church (five, including "I
Would Not Live Away"). Much earlier, Muhlenberg had edited a
hymnal, *Church Poetry*,[10] which included one of three poems other
than the "Star-Spangled Banner" known to have been published during Key's lifetime. It was "Hymn" ("Lord, with glowing heart I'd
praise thee"). Number 139 in the collection, it appeared without a
title and without attribution.

Most of the sacred pieces in *Poems* were tenderly wrought el-
egies Key wrote for his relatives and friends. One example is a
moving epitaph Key wrote in 1809 for the Reverend Johannes J.
Sayrs, first rector of St. John's Church in Georgetown. In it Key
praised his pastor in terms that reflected his own spiritual values:

> Here once stood forth a man who from the world,
> Though bright in aspect to the youthful eye,
> Turned with affection ardent to his God,

15

*Portrait of Key by C. Gregory Stapko hanging in
St. John's Church, Georgetown Parish, Washington
D.C. Author's photo.*

And lived and died an humble minister
Of His benignant purposes to man.[11]

The blank-verse sonnet was carved on a white marble tablet
and placed at the grave site. Ever mindful of the need to fight the
deadly sin of pride, Key did not wish his name to appear on or near
the plaque, and it doesn't to this day. The tablet, brought up from
the crypt when the church was enlarged in 1843,[12] is now affixed to
the west wall of the sanctuary.

Sacred lyrics reflected Key's concern with the destiny of men
and women and their relationship to God. That concern also surfaced in Key's role in black colonization. In 1816 Key was a founding member of the American Colonization Society, formed "to promote and execute a plan for colonizing (with their consent) the free

people of color residing in our country, in Africa, or such other places as Congress shall deem most expedient." Key headed a list of twelve "managers," who did most of the real work of the society. Three of the other managers were members of the clergy.[13] The society's founders viewed colonization as the only viable solution to the vexing and delicate question of slavery, but ridicule, personal calumny, and increasing opposition beset them. As one of the most conspicuous leaders of the movement, Key suffered the scorn of Southerners who identified him with abolitionists, and the derision of abolitionists who regarded him as a temporizer. Like his close friends and fellow organizers of the society, the Reverend (later bishop) William Meade and the Reverend Robert Finley, Key firmly believed that his humane purpose had the approval of Providence.

The Colonization Society was only one of many organizations devoted to the betterment of humanity that Key assisted over the years both with his labors and with his purse. Among others were Georgetown's Lancaster Society for the free education of the poor, the General Theological Seminary in Alexandria, and the Domestic and Foreign Missionary Society. But, as one might surmise, Key gave the church his most consistent and enthusiastic support. He served well all four parishes he joined but most notably Christ Church, Georgetown (then an independent municipality), with which he was affiliated from 1817 to the mid-1830s. He then moved with his family to Washington City, where he joined Trinity Church, which is no longer in existence. Key was appointed to the Christ Church committee on site and planning for a new building and was selected to attend conventions of the Maryland diocese five times between 1821 and 1828. In 1828 he was elected to the governing body of the church and served as a vestryman for the remainder of his time in Georgetown.[14] For these and other indefatigable efforts in support of Christ Church, Key received special recognition at the consecration of the new building on the exact site of the old in 1887. At the ceremony, the rector, Reverend Albert Stuart, referred directly to the three stained-glass windows dedicated to Key: Moses and Aaron, representing the patriotism of the ancient people of God, and Miriam, the prophetess, singing her triumph song. The middle window bears the inscription to Key with the date of the first organizational meeting of the eight founders on 10 November 1817.

Beyond the local parish, Key also was chosen to be a delegate to every General Convention of the Protestant Episcopal Church

The center of three stained glass windows in memory of Key at the Christ Church, O Street, Washington D.C. Courtesy of the Church.

(held triennially) from 1814 to 1826, and he attended all but the first. On more than one occasion, he helped reconcile the contending factions of the high and low churches, or the formalist and evangelical branches. He belonged to the evangelical branch which relied on Scripture and individual conscience, while the high party generally attached more weight to church traditions.

Key had such strong feelings of fellowship in the Episcopal Church that he twice thought of entering the ministry. In the spring of 1814—when the courts were closed because of the war and his law practice was practically at a standstill—Key was invited to become associate rector of St. Paul's Church in Baltimore by the Reverend Dr. James Kemp. After much soul-searching, Key declined the position, explaining that if he were to enter the ministry on such handsome terms he might be thought to "act under the influence of unworthy inducements, and thus the cause of religion in some measure might receive injury."[15]

Key held fast to the belief that life on earth is transitory and that "the soul has no home" here; he never departed from the canon that true believers praise God best by participating fully in the activities of their chosen church and doing good works. In the Bristol College speech of 1834, Key reminded his youthful audience that they should, in the words of Paul's Epistle to the Ephesians, "work with hands so that they may have to give to him that needeth." He said further that, for the faithful follower of Christ, one of the richest blessings of life and "the greatest of all luxuries" was that of doing good.[16]

Guided by such beliefs and his low-church orientation, Key habitually performed acts of Christian charity. In October of 1818, for example, when a distraught mother brought her ailing infant to Key's Bridge Street house with an urgent plea that he baptize it, the lay leader granted her request. Afterward, Dr. Kemp, then bishop, severely reprimanded him for performing this sacrament, writing that Key had assumed "an agency in the affairs of the church beyond the limits of a layman."

For many years Key assisted the Reverend Walter Dulany Addison in the work of St. John's Parish, visiting the sick in hospitals and prisoners in jail. He even held up the infirm pastor's arms so that he might pronounce benediction. On Sunday afternoons in the years around 1820 Key often visited St. Paul's Church in Rock Creek, which lacked a minister, to repeat the sermon that Reverend

Reuel Keith of Christ Church had preached in the morning.[17] In Key's best-known psalm, still appearing in Protestant psalters and beginning, "Lord, with glowing heart I'd praise thee," he underscored the importance of striving to live in conformity with the Christian ethic of good works:

> Lord! this bosom's ardent feeling
>   Vainly would my lips express;
> -
> And, since words can never measure,
>   Let my life show forth thy praise.[18]

> We the members of the Vestry of St. John's Church, Georgetown, fully sensible how important it is that the services of our church should be duly and regularly performed, and as our Rector, W. D. Addison, is, through indisposition, unable to go through the same, we therefore request you to appoint Francis S. Key as Lay Reader, whose Talents and Piety, and soundness in the Faith, render him apt and meet to exercise the office thus reposed in him. We are, Rt. Rev. Sir, yours very respectfully,
>
> W. D. Addison.

1816 petition by Rev. Addison requesting the appointment of Key as a Lay Reader in St. John's Church. Courtesy of the Addison family.

One of these acts of benevolence brought the thirty-five-year-old lawyer and churchman to the Patapsco River on the night of 13-14 September 1814—an errand of mercy to rescue Dr. William Beanes from the hold of a British warship. After the doctor's friends in Prince George's County had failed to win his release from the British, temporarily headquartered at Benedict, Richard West rushed to Georgetown to ask for his brother-in-law's help. Key was well acquainted with the physician, who was described in an official letter at the time as being "far advanced in life, infirm, and unaccustomed to privation."[19]

Writing to his father on 2 September, Key voiced doubt that he would succeed in getting Dr. Beanes released. Nevertheless, he volunteered for the task. After obtaining approval from President James Madison and supporting documents from General John Mason for undertaking what promised to be an arduous and hazardous endeavor, Key—accompanied by prisoner-of-war exchange officer John Stuart Skinner—set sail from Baltimore down the Chesapeake Bay in search of the British fleet, which by then had gotten under way.[20]

When Key returned to Baltimore on the 16th, he carried with him the crinkled paper on which he had jotted down the lines of a nearly completed poem. Given his devoutly Christian character, he was probably most gratified by the success of the mission. Together with Skinner, he had won the good doctor's release from British captivity and enabled Beanes to return to his residence in Upper Marlboro in plenty of time for the doctor and his wife, Sarah, to attend Sunday morning services at the Trinity Episcopal Church, where he was senior warden.

Notes

1. Weybright, *Spangled Banner: The Story of Francis Scott Key (New York: Farrar and Rinehart Inc. 1935)*, pp. 1-2.

2. Francis Scott Key, *The Power of Literature and Its Connexion with Religion,* [Bristol, Conn.]: Bristol College, 1834, p. 4. See also Fred Somkin, *Unquiet Eagle: Memory and Desire in the Idea of American Freedom, 1815-1860* (Ithaca, N.Y.: Cornell University Press, 1967), p. 170. Speaking to the Maryland Historical Society at the end of the nineteenth century, Lawrence C. Wroth noted that the idea of Jehovah, the God of Battles, leading the righteous to victory, had been an article of faith to most men and women of Key's generation. See Lawrence C. Wroth, "Francis Scott Key as a Churchman," *Maryland Historical Magazine*, 4 (1909): 154-70.

3. Francis Scott Key-Smith (1872-1951), an overseas veteran of World War I who later rose to the rank of lieutenant colonel in the Army Reserve, practiced law in Washington, D.C. for more than fifty years. He made a kind of second career of speaking and writing about his ancestor and working to perpetuate his fame. He also wrote poetry and was, like his forebear, keenly interested in literature. In a biography of his great-grandfather he included a memorial tribute, "Our Patriot," containing the lines: "He's gone to meet his God on high, / His duty here well done" (*Francis Scott Key*, p. 8). Only a few years before his death, in a letter to Dr. H. Paul Caemmerer, President of the

Columbia Historical Society of Washington, D.C., Key-Smith offered to present an ambitious lecture, "Poetry and Poets," which he described as one of the best things he had ever done, and further said he wanted also to deliver the paper at a meeting of the Maryland Historical Society (Key vertical file, Columbia Historical Society, Washington, D.C.). There is no record of his having ever given the reading before either of the societies.

4. Francis Scott Key-Smith, "The Story of the Star-Spangled Banner," *Current History*, 32 (1930): 270-71; see also Key-Smith, "Fort McHenry and the 'Star-Spangled Banner,'" *The Republic Magazine*, 1(April 1908): 20. For a contrary martial view of "The Star-Spangled Banner," see Henry Watterson, *The Compromises of Life and Other Lectures and Addresses* (New York: Fox, Duffield and Co., 1903), p. 334.

5. Harold R. and Beta K. Manakee, p. 12.

6. For the text of Key's Alexandria address, see Edward S. Delaplaine, *Francis Scott Key*, pp. 105-15.

7. William Wilberforce, *A Practical View of the Prevailing Religious System of Professed Christians in the Higher and Middle Classes, Contrasted with Real Christianity*, 2nd ed. (London: T. Codell and W. Davies, 1797), pp. 395-96.

8. Key, *Poems*, p. 97. The editor of *Poems*, Henry V. D. Johns (1803-1859), was ordained a priest around 1826 in St. John's Church, Georgetown.

9. Charles Dexter Cleveland, ed., *Lyra Sacra Americana or Gems from American Sacred Poetry* (New York: Charles Scribner and Co., 1868).

10. William August Muhlenberg, ed., *Church Poetry: Being Portions of Psalms in Verse and Hymns Suited to the Festivals and Feasts, and Various Occasions of the Church* (Philadelphia: P.S. Porter and Co., 1823), pp. 208-9. Singing of "Hymn" (no. 150 in the Protestant songbook) concluded Key's funeral service in Christ Church, Cincinnati, on 9 January 1843. Key's former pastor, the Rev. Brooke, conducted the service (Brooke, p. 14).

11. Key, *Poems*, p. 132.

12. Mary Mitchell, *A Short History of St. John's Church Georgetown from 1796 to 1968,* p. 7.

13. For the object of the American Colonization Society, its first officers and managers, and the duties of the principals, see *The First Annual Report of the American Society for Colonizing the People of Color . . . and the Proceedings of the Society in the City of Washington on the First Day of January 1818* (Washington, D.C.: D. Rapine, 1818).

14. On Key's contribution to this parish and on the dedication of the three stained glass windows commemorating Key, see Albert R. Stuart, A Sermon delivered in Christ Church, Georgetown, D.C. on the morning of the Third Sunday in Advent, 1887, p. 10.

15. Key to Kemp, 4 and 28 April 1814. Facsimiles of these and other letters and papers from the Maryland Diocesan Archives, Maryland Historical Society, Baltimore, were supplied to the author by Glenn A. Metzdorf, archivist of Christ Church, with the consent of the rector, the Rev. Sanford Garner.

16. Key, *Power of Literature*, pp. 7, 17.

17. The affair of the disputed baptism is in the Key-Kemp correspondence, 12 and 17 October 1818, Maryland Diocesan Archives. For Key's help to Rev. Addison, see Wroth, p. 164. Key's repeating of Rev. Keith's sermon is mentioned in a letter, Metzdorf to Larsen, 2 Aug. 1985. Norman L. Larsen was the President of the Francis Scott Key Foundation.

18. Key, *Poems*, p. 172.

19. General John Mason, U.S. commissary general of prisoners, to Major General Robert Ross, British army commander, 2 September 1814, quoted in Svejda, p. 61. This letter, hand-carried by Key for delivery to Ross, formally requested the release of Dr. Beanes.

20. See Francis Scott Key to John Ross Key, 2 September 1814, in Filby and Howard, p. 151. In an unpublished paper read before the Maryland Historical Society at Baltimore on 14 Oct. 1929, Key-Smith drew attention to the hardships and difficulties of Key's undertaking. They included a day's journey via horse-drawn stagecoach over rough roads between Georgetown and Baltimore, and then a sailing by packet to catch up to the British fleet not far from the mouth of the Patuxent River (Francis Scott Key-Smith, "Francis Scott Key and the National Anthem," pp. 13-14 (Md. Hist. Soc. Ms. 2008). Another descendant, Anna Key Bartow, noted that Key purposely kept his wife ignorant of the peril of the mission, knowing that such knowledge would increase her anxieties for him ("Recollections of Francis Scott Key," *Modern Culture*, 12, No. 3 (Nov. 1900): 206).

Chapter 3

Soldier-Patriot and Slaveholder

At least two facets of Francis Scott Key's real life appear at first glance to conflict somewhat with the idealized image he was given as the author of "The Star-Spangled Banner." They merit attention if one is to get a fair view of the man behind the legend. These twofold aspects have to do with Key's attitude toward the War of 1812, including his own service in the military, and his position vis-à-vis slaves and slavery.

Key regarded war as the scourge of mankind and believed fervently in peaceful means of settling disputes among nations.[1] After President James Madison, under pressure from the Republican majority in Congress (the so-called War Hawks led by Calhoun, Clay, and Langdon Cheves), formally committed the United States to the conflict with Great Britain by his proclamation of 19 June 1812, Key predicted dire consequences for the nation; he believed it would suffer divine retribution. For example, he specifically attributed the depression that began after the war started to the God of Wrath who was chastising the American people for their wickedness.[2] Key's strong repugnance toward war on religious grounds made it rather surprising that he eventually participated in the war as a member of the military and that he penned a song that many still consider a glorification of war.

Besides his religious antipathy toward war, Key was totally unsympathetic to the aims of those in Congress and their supporters, mainly in the South and West, who clamored for war with Great Britain. The early claims that the war party used to justify hostilities—stopping the impressment of American sailors to serve on ships of the Royal Navy and ending England's seizure of American merchant ships on the high seas—soon gave way to more aggressive aims. The foremost of the goals was to wrest Canada from Great

Britain. Although this campaign eventually failed, American troops in April of 1813 captured and pillaged York (now Montreal), the provincial capital of Canada, burning down two houses of the Canadian Parliament. In October of the same year an American invasion, which aimed to capture York, was abandoned when winter began.[3]

News of the withdrawal of American Forces under General Wade Hampton to Plattsburg, New York, prompted Key to write a letter to his close friend, John Randolph, a congressman from Virginia who also strongly opposed the war. In this letter Key expressed joy at the news of the withdrawal, saying that he would rather see the American flag that he so much revered lowered in disgrace than have it stand for persecution and dishonor. He added that one could construe as treasonable his hopes for the continued safety of the Canadian city, but if so he would glory in the name of traitor. He wrote of Patrick Henry, who had uttered similar sentiments when more conservative members of the Virginia House of Burgesses accused him of treason for making menacing allusions to King George III, whose Parliament had passed the odious Stamp Act in 1765.[4]

Despite the fact that Key thought the war with England was unchristian and ill-advised, he did not carry his moral and political scruples so far that they inhibited resistance to an actual invasion of American soil by the enemy. After all, his father, John Ross Key, had also taken up arms in defense of his country against a foreign expeditionary force during the Revolutionary War. Key volunteered for militia service late in the war, only when his native Maryland was directly threatened. During the summer of 1813, a British squadron was ravaging towns along the Chesapeake Bay, presaging an attack against the capital and adjacent Georgetown.

Francis Scott Key, from the original supposed to have been cut by him.

A brief recap of Key's military service reveals that, despite the heroic status that he now enjoys in retrospect, his short stints in the Army deserve few if any accolades.

Key's first tour was with the Georgetown Field Artillery Company, a militia unit hastily assembled by Major George Peter of Georgetown, then a flourishing community of some 4,000 residents adjoining the new Federal City. Key lived in Georgetown with his wife, Mary, and their family and practiced law. From 15 to 26 July 1813, he served as a matross, a soldier who assisted the gunner in loading, firing, and sponging the guns.[5] Key lacked aptitude for this necessary but mundane task. Fortunately, the company was not required to engage in any action with the enemy.

The next summer, with courts adjourned and his law practice virtually at a standstill, Key reentered the militia on 18 June 1814, now as an officer with the rank of lieutenant and quartermaster. (The promotion required no change in the artillery uniform that all militiamen were required to provide on their own. His wife merely had to sew epaulets on the shoulders.)[6] With his company Key proceeded toward the Patuxent River. The British fleet had anchored along the shores of the river. Much to the relief of Major Peter and his lieutenant, His Majesty, King George III's flotilla had decided to turn around and start down the river. The American commander promptly ordered the Light Artillery back to Georgetown, where Key was discharged on 1 July 1814.[7] One of Key's biographers characterized him as an ineffective quartermaster. He apparently lacked the aggressive truculence that the times called for in order successfully to commandeer horses and provisions from the reluctant farmers.

In another letter to Randolph, Key recounted in a light vein the experience that occurred during the June fortnight of campaigning in the vicinity of Benedict in Charles County, Maryland. The enemy was present but not in contact with Major Peter's artillery. In one instance, Key was pitched over his horse's head into the river, with no harm resulting other than the near ruination of his uniform. In another, he was accidentally struck in the face by a piece of salt pork, suffering no injury except to his pride.[8]

The conclusion of Key's military career, such as it was, happened under grimmer circumstances. In August of 1814, he volunteered to act as an aide to General Walter Smith, whom General William Winder had put in charge of a reserve force of Washington and Georgetown militia to help defend the capital from an expected enemy assault. The British had openly declared their intention to lay waste to the city in retaliation for American forces torching York earlier.

By 24 August the enemy had arrived at Bladensburg, a village on the eastern branch of the Potomac, only five miles from Washington. General Winder had been mobilizing troops around Bladensburg in the hope that he could stem the British march on the capital. Key was assigned the task of directing the regiments to their allocated positions in the field.[9] Owing to confusion, divided command responsibility, and the militia's inexperience in the face of aggression by hardened British regulars, the Battle of Bladensburg ended after a couple of hours in a route of the American defenders— the so-called Bladensburg races. The British now had a virtually unopposed path to the nearby capital, where the forces under Major General Robert Ross and Rear Admiral George Cockburn proceeded to lay waste to the city. They set fire to the Capitol, the President's mansion (not yet painted white), the Treasury Building, the War Office, and buildings housing war supplies, but they did not molest the civilian population (although the British commanders and some of their aides did dine on the hastily prepared meal Mr. Madison and Dolley, his wife, had left behind in their hurried departure).

While details of Key's activities on that afternoon at Bladensburg are very sparse, an "Inquiry Respecting the Capture of Washington by the British," now in the Rare Book Room of the Library of Congress, imputed blame for poor disposition of forces both to "F. S. Key" and one "Colonel Monroe"[10]—that is, James Monroe, Secretary of State, who succeeded Madison as President in 1817.

It probably would be unrealistic to have expected Key to excel as a soldier. Already in his mid-thirties, a country squire and an office man by profession, he was ill-fitted to life in the field. Moreover, he had no formal military training. On balance, one cannot fairly fault Key as a soldier-patriot when he, unlike many of his compatriots in the field at Bladensburg, did not panic and run in the face of superior enemy fire power.[11]

These experiences highlight the disparity between the popular romanticized concept of Key as a soldier-patriot and his strong misgivings about the righteousness of the war.

The second possible discrepancy between Key's ideals and his practices emerges when one compares sentiments Key expressed in his famous anthem and with his position and conduct in relation to slaves and slavery. Each of the four stanzas of "The Star-Spangled Banner" ends, as everyone knows, with the ringing second line of the chorus—"O'er the land of the free and the home of the brave."

Yet for the slaves who mainly took complete charge of Key's country plantation, Terra Rubra—or "Pike Creek" as the family called it—and his large household in Georgetown, America was hardly the land of the free. Like most of his neighbors in Frederick (now Carroll) County, Maryland, where Key grew up, and like those in Georgetown, Key owned a large number of slaves. Some of these had been transferred to him and his wife, Mary, by their parents; the rest they later inherited from their parents. Having spent his childhood and youth with many of the slaves on his father's estate, he held them in close affection. Indeed, as with his eleven children, he had the reputation of being overindulgent with them. One exception to this permissiveness was his strict requirement that they attend the daily family prayers he conducted.[12]

Key clearly expressed his position on the highly charged issue of slaves and slaveholding in a written reply to a questionnaire mailed to him by the Reverend Benjamin Tappan in 1838, when Key was nearing sixty. Reverend Tappan represented the Congregational Church in the North. At this time Key was a nationally known lay leader of the Protestant Episcopal Church. In his reply to Reverend Tappan, Key contended that the Bible neither expressly permitted nor prohibited slavery. He asserted further that God sanctioned slavery if it was practiced in accordance with the Golden Rule but did not if it was for such as buying and selling slaves for profit. In reply to the fourth question of the questionnaire, unfortunately Key expressed a view common in his time but completely unacceptable now, namely, that the Negroes constituted "a distinct and inferior race."

Also in response to Reverend Tappan, Key said that he had emancipated seven of his slaves but was concerned that once they became old and infirm then they would suffer greatly.[13] This solicitude for the fate of freed slaves was undoubtedly one reason that he did not liberate more of them.

Mary Tayloe Lloyd Key, from a miniature by Robert Field. Library of Congress.

On this matter of emancipation, a Circuit Court decision applicable to the Federal District held that the courts could nullify any provision in a master's will conferring freedom upon a slave if the slave was over forty-five. The grounds for this ruling was the probability of such a person becoming a public charge.[14] Mindful perhaps of his decision, Key expressly stipulated in his will that slaves still held in the family were to belong to Mary.

As a member of the bar, Key conformed to the shared agreement of the legal profession not to make exceptions among clients. This seemed to override any compunction he might have had about accepting as clients slaveholders who wanted to maintain possession of their property. During the 1812 term of Court, for example, Key represented Hezekiah Wood, a slaveowner, in opposing the freedom of children of a free mulatto woman. After losing the case at Circuit Court level, Key won it on appeal to the United States Supreme Court, Chief Justice John Marshall presiding. On the other hand, Key was not averse to taking on, sometimes without fee, blacks claiming legal rights to freedom.[15]

During the first half of the nineteenth century, many people thought a valid solution to the slavery problem was colonization—emancipating slaves who were willing to go to colonies established for them in Africa. Key strongly opposed outright abolition and favored colonization just as Abraham Lincoln did in a signed statement he made in 1837 while he was a member of the Illinois legislature. Lincoln later changed his view on both positions, but Key never did. In his last pronouncement on the subject of slavery, an address before the American Colonization Society in Washington, D.C., on 9 May 1842, Key spoke eloquently in favor of the resolution urging the United States to promote commerce with Africa, suppress the slave trade, and protect the American colonies of blacks then established on the west coast of Africa.[16] Key must have had considerable moral courage to maintain his unceasing advocacy of the objectives of the Society that he had helped found in 1816.

The dilemma that Key and all the other slaveholders of more than 100,000 slaves in Maryland faced was expressed by the Reverend John T. Brooke at the memorial service following Key's death on 11 January 1843. In his sermon on 29 January, at Christ Church in Cincinnati, Reverend Brooke devoted some time to a discussion of the slavery issue and his former parishioner's attitude toward it. He told the mourners in the congregation that both Key and his friend, the Reverend William Meade, a senior bishop at a Virginia church,

"The Key House" by John Ross Key (1832-1920), dated 1908.
Oil on paper. John Ross was the grandson of Francis Scott Key.
According to Key's great-grandson, Francis Scott Key-Smith, the
painting is accurate in every detail but one: the grade of the
fronting street being lower in the 1800s than when John Ross did
the picture; five or six steps, and windows lighting the basement
dining room then appeared between the street grade and the
entrance level of the home. The mansion, situated on M Street
west of the present Francis Scott Key Bridge, was demolished in
1949 to make way for the Whitehurst Freeway. The original
painting is in the Diplomatic Reception Rooms of the U.S.
Department of State. A framed copy in color, retouched and
autographed by the artist, hangs at the top of the stairs in the
Home and Museum of Chief Justice Roger B. Taney on South
Bentz Street in Frederick, Md. Diplomatic Reception Rooms, U.S.
Department of State, Washington, D.C.

like all pious people, deplored the existence of slavery as a mighty
evil. But even though they were aware of the difficulties and dan-
gers connected with slavery, they could see no public instrument
with which they could work hopefully, safely, and legally, or even
scripturally, against it except African colonization of those willing
to go. "And if ever a man was a true friend to the African race,"
Brooke asserted, "that man was Francis Scott Key." Reverend Brooke

specifically referred to the legal services that Key extended gratuitously to those Negroes in trouble, "pressing their right to the extent of the law, and ready to brave odium or even personal danger in their behalf."[17]

In conclusion, two aspects of Key's beliefs and conduct—his less than enthusiastic response to his President's call to arms and his holding of slaves—may seem to lower him in the eyes of posterity. Key probably would not have demurred. As a devout Christian he would have been the first to confess susceptibility to error. "All one can do," as he wrote in a letter of 20 March 1812, to be given to his children after his death, "is to pray and strive to do everything right and to shun everything wrong."[18] The Reverend Brooke noted in his sermon that Key was no more immune to human fallibility than anyone else. Early in his laudatory oration, the rector stated that Key's character was unique, so much so, he added, "that strangers and mere passing acquaintances sometimes misapprehend both his excellence and his failings. For he was not faultless. He was a *man*—not an *angel*!"[19]

Notes

1. Weybright, p. 37; Delaplaine, *Francis Scott Key*, p. 137; Donald M. Dozer, *Portrait of the Free State: A History of Maryland* (Cambridge, Md.: Tidewater Publishers, 1976), p. 335.

2. Delaplaine, *Francis Scott Key*, pp. 96-97.

3. Henry L. Coles, *The War of 1812* (Chicago: The University of Chicago Press, 1965), p. 147.

4. Delaplaine, *Francis Scott Key*, pp. 99-100.

5. Weybright, p. 69.

6. Ibid., p. 84

7. Delaplaine, *Francis Scott Key*, pp. 130-31.

8. Weybright, pp. 86-87

9. Delaplaine, *Francis Scott Key*, p. 137.

10. Ibid., p. 138 n.1.

11. Charles Francis Stein, *Our National Anthem The Star-Spangled Banner* (Baltimore, Md.: Whitmore Park Federal Savings and Loan Assoc., 1964), p. 17; Joseph E. Jensen, "66 Years Ago This Month . . . William Beanes the Doctor behind 'The Star-Spangled Banner,'" *Maryland State Medical Journal* (Sept. 1980): 65, n. 11.

12. Key-Smith, *Francis Scott Key*, p. 16.

13. Key's responses to Rev. Tappan's questionnaire are drawn from Delaplaine, *Francis Scott Key*, pp. 446-50.

14. Walter C. Clephane, "The Local Aspects of Slavery in the District of Columbia," *Records of the Columbia Historical Society of Washington, D. C.*, 3 (1900): 229-30.

15. Delaplaine, *Francis Scott Key*, pp. 76-77.

16. Ibid., pp. 451-57.

17. Brooke, p. 13.

18. Key to "Polly" [wife, Mary] and "My Dear Children," 20 March 1812 from Portobasco (transcript in vertical file, "Francis Scott Key," Enoch Pratt Free Library, Baltimore, Md.)

19. Brooke, p. 7.

Chapter 4

William Beanes:
The Doctor Who Rode Backward Into History

Shortly after midnight on 28 August 1814, a detachment from the British cavalry galloped up to an imposing residence in the little town of Upper Marlboro in Maryland. Dismounting quickly, they stormed into the house of a sixty-five-year-old physician and surgeon by the name of William Beanes. They pulled him unceremoniously out of bed, and set him, only half clothed, on a sorry mule for a thirty-five-mile ride over rough roads to Benedict, Maryland. Benedict lay at the mouth of the Patuxent River where it flowed into the Chesapeake Bay. It was the temporary headquarters of the British Expeditionary Force awaiting embarkation for their next campaign in the War of 1812.

Who was this Dr. Beanes? And why was a civilian medico, described in an official letter of the time as "far advanced in life, infirm, and unaccustomed to privations,"[1] treated so rudely and harshly by his martial captors, with worse yet to come? Further, why should anyone be concerned about this venerable practitioner of medicine more than 175 years later?

Dr. William Beanes, the third of his name and representing the fourth generation of his family to reside in America, was born at Brooke Ridge in Prince George's County, Maryland, in 1749.[2] Little is known of his early life but since his parents were large landholders, he doubtless grew up in an environment of relative ease and comfort. Because there was no medical college in the colonies at the time, he almost certainly studied under an experienced practitioner in his area.[3]

In the early 1770s, the colonists were growing increasingly resistant to the efforts of Great Britain to strengthen its control over them. The young Dr. Beanes joined a local committee formed to carry out the "resolves" of the first Continental Congress to protest against odious taxes and to prepare for armed opposition. When fighting broke out at Concord and Lexington in April of 1775, William Beanes left Maryland to join the staff of the new general hospital that the Continental Congress had established in Philadelphia. He spent a year or more there tending wounded soldiers of the Continental Army.[4] There is no listing of his name, however, in the official register of the Armed Forces.[5] Accordingly, unlike his better-known contemporaries, Doctors Benjamin Rush and William Skippen, he never was actually commissioned in Washington's forces. An entry, however, in the *Journal of Maryland* for 4 September 1777, recorded his appointment in the Maryland Marching Militia. Dr. Beanes may have even served in his state's volunteer forces earlier. William L. Marbury, in *The Patriotic Marylander* for September 1914, told of hearing his great aunt, a niece of Dr. Beanes, say that Uncle Beanes and her grandfather, Colonel Luke Marbury, were engaged with the Maryland troops at the Battle of Long Island and were among the few to escape on 30 August 1776, after the disastrous battle, by swimming across Long Island Sound.[6]

As the War of Independence wound to a close, Dr. Beanes returned to Prince George's County. In 1779 he built a mansion on what is now Elm Street in Upper Marlboro, which was known as "Academy Hill."[7] His practice thrived, enabling him to acquire several farms and the local grist mill. His professional reputation spread far beyond Prince George's County. Accordingly, when the Medical and Chirurgical Faculty of the State of Maryland was established, he was one of the 101 incorporators and a member of the first examining board. He attended the initial meeting, which was held in Annapolis in June, 1799.[8] The preamble to the charter granted by the General Assembly stated that the purpose of the society was "promoting and disseminating medical and chirurgical knowledge throughout the State," and protecting its citizens from "risking their lives in the hands of ignorant practitioners or pretenders to the healing art."[9] The Faculty, now known in short as "Chi-Med," but with its official name unchanged, has more than fulfilled the hopes of its founders. Housed in a splendid facility in Baltimore, it is now one of the most flourishing and progressive of state medical societies, and a component of the American Medical Association.

Artist's conception of the three American hostages—Dr. Beanes, Key, and Col. Skinner—on the truce-boat in Baltimore harbor on the morning of 14 September 1814. This mural by R. McGill Mackall at the Homewood Retirement Center (formerly Francis Scott Key Hotel) in Frederick, Md., shows Key in the process of composing the future National Anthem. Author's photo.

Up to the time Dr. Beanes helped organize Chi-Med at the age of fifty, there was nothing remarkable about the story of this physician and planter of Upper Marlboro. But a decade and a half later, at the end of August 1814, when the British troopers aroused him from his peaceful slumber, he began a ride literally backward into history! For then his captors, heedless of his rank and gray hairs, added insult to injury by turning his face to the mule's tail. With bare feet tied under the animal's belly, he was herded throughout the night and the next day to where the invading army was encamped. From there he was shipped as a brig prisoner on the flagship HMS *Tonnant* down the Chesapeake Bay.[10] Indeed, once aboard ship, his captors threatened to hang him from the nearest yardarm,[11] or send him to Halifax in the Canadian province of Nova Scotia to stand trial for treason.

What heinous offense, one hastens to ask, had this seemingly innocuous medical practitioner committed in the eyes of the British commanders, Major General Robert Ross and Rear Admiral George Cockburn, to warrant such drastic measures? There is no wholly agreed-upon answer to this question, but it may clarify the issue to recount briefly the events that transpired prior to the doctor's seizure and imprisonment. According to the British infantry officer present at the time, Lieutenant George Robert Gleig, who kept a diary later published as *A Subaltern in America*, Dr. Beanes was the only inhabitant remaining in the town of Marlboro on 22 August 1814, when the British entered it on their way to raid the American capital. Since Academy Hill was the finest residence, the English commanders, Ross and Cockburn, almost automatically selected it as their temporary headquarters. General Ross and some of his officers stayed overnight. Whether Dr. Beanes willingly acquiesced in these arrangements is not certain. Being alone and without military backup, he had little choice in the matter. In any event, it was greatly to his personal advantage to play the part of the gracious host. Gleig, who subsequently rose to become Chaplain-General of the British Army, recalled, "There was nothing about his house or farm to which he made us not heartily welcome," adding pointedly, "and the wily emigrant was no loser by his civility."[12]

Gleig meant that, in exchange for sharing his food, his best tobacco, and fine wine from his well-stocked cellar, the doctor received protection from British guards stationed around his grounds and outbuildings to prevent depredations by their troops.[13] In addition, they paid him the full value of provisions, forage, and even horses that he provided. Then, in this atmosphere of mutual cordiality, Dr. Beanes told the occupiers that he opposed the war, that he had migrated some twenty years earlier from North Britain (completely untrue), and that he still regarded England as his mother country. Gleig found these statements by Dr. Beanes quite credible; he said Beanes still retained his Scottish brogue and "seemed readily disposed to treat us as friends."[14] He did not have to add that if Beanes had emigrated from Great Britain, under British law he would remain a citizen of that nation. Ironically then, as it turned out, Dr. Beanes' protestations and his excess of hospitality later contributed to his undoing. But there would not have been any harsh consequences for him if he had not taken certain deliberate actions less than a week later.

When the British came back from burning public buildings in Washington on 24-25 August—in retribution for American forces having set fire the previous year to York, the provincial Canadian capital—stragglers and deserters from the British Army plundered the countryside for several days. On 28 August soldiers of the withdrawing army broke into the grounds of Dr. Beanes' estate and brusquely demanded food and drink. At the time the disruption occurred, Dr. Beanes was entertaining a former governor of Maryland, Robert Bowie, a fellow-physician, and a prominent citizen, Philip Weems, in his spring garden house. Versions of what happened next differ, but what is certain is that Dr. Beanes and some other citizens arrested the stragglers and had them thrown into the county jail. One managed to escape, however, and reported to his superiors an exaggerated story concerning the violent treatment accorded them by the doctor and his accomplices.[15] In response, General Ross sent back a detachment to arrest Dr. Beanes and two of his guests. Dr. Hill and Weems were subsequently released but Beanes was retained in strict confinement.[16]

Friends of the physician lost no time in rallying to effect his release. The first to take concrete steps in this direction was William Thornton, M.D., head of the Patuxent Office and Architect of the Capitol. On 30 August, he approached James Monroe, then Secretary of State, and John Mason, Commissary General of Prisoners. They gave him encouragement but no commitment to action.[17] The next day, Richard West, a patient of Dr. Beanes and the husband of Key's wife's elder sister, hastened to British headquarters at Benedict. Armed with a pass from Governor Levin Winder of Maryland, he carried with him some necessaries for Dr. Beanes and a dispatch from the governor addressed to General Ross. The dispatch attested to the probity of the doctor and asked that, on the grounds of "justice and humanity," he be permitted to return speedily to his wife and friends.[18] Despite Winder's plea, General Ross adamantly refused to budge. On 1 September, West set out for Georgetown, where Key lived and had his law office. As a District of Columbia militiaman under Major George Peter, Key had only a week before been with Monroe and other government officials on the battlefield of Bladensburg, just northeast of the capital. Here, poorly led and ill-trained American forces tried in vain to stem the advance of British regulars on Washington during several hours of fighting on 24 August 1814.[19] Upon learning of the serious plight of his friend, "poor old Dr. Beanes," as he later termed him in a letter,[20] Key immediately secured permission from President James Madison to visit the

British fleet under a flag of truce and negotiate directly with General Ross for the physician's release. Madison referred Key to General Mason, who then formally delegated him and John S. Skinner, prisoner-of-exchange officer for the United States, already known to the British command, to proceed with the mission.[21] The two Americans took with them a strong letter dated 2 September from General Mason, in which he charged that the arrest and incarceration of Dr. Beanes, "unarmed and entirely of non-combatant character," constituted a "departure from the known usages of civilized warfare."[22]

Key and Skinner, in their cartel boat flying a white flag, caught up with the British fleet on 7 September in the Chesapeake Bay. When the two men were conveyed on board the HMS *Tonnant*, General Ross and his staff received them cordially. In a private meeting that night with Skinner, Ross agreed to free Dr. Beanes.[23] He also replied to General Mason in a letter that he asked Skinner to take back. In no mind to mince words, General Ross declared that Dr. Beanes had acted hostilely toward certain soldiers under his command by making them prisoners, when they were proceeding to rejoin the army. He went on to say that he had spoken to Dr. Beanes, who attempted to justify his conduct. Whatever the latter's explanation was at that time, it failed to satisfy the commanding general because he ended his short letter by saying that he would order Dr. Beanes released and added significantly, "not from an opinion of his not being justifiably detained, nor from any sentiment of merit . . . but purely in proof of the obligation which I feel for the attention with which the wounded have been treated."[24]

This last acknowledged the care American physicians and surgeons had given to British soldiers wounded and left behind at both Bladensburg and Washington. Of these, Dr. James Ewell of Carrel Row in Washington, was especially assiduous in helping enemy survivors, making a full round of dressings before evening on 25 August. Of particular interest is that two of the convalescent Britons whom he treated learned later that Dr. Beanes had been arrested. They then wrote a letter to General Ross asking that he give favorable consideration to any matters brought before him by the Americans.[25] It was this letter—and others from recovering enemy troops, carried by Key and Skinner on their rescue errand—that turned the tide in Ross' previously consistent refusal to free Dr. Beanes.[26]

Did Dr. Beanes himself render medical aid to the British? Key's great-grandson, Francis Scott Key-Smith, writing in 1911, asserted that he did. Statements to this effect were repeated in the two later biographies of Key,[27] but no documentary nor other evidence has been brought forward to substantiate the contention that Dr. Beanes personally rendered professional services to English sick and injured. Certainly, had he done so, the British would have been much more inclined to resolve in his favor any reservations they might have had as to his behavior toward the stragglers. No mention is made of Beanes' medical assistance to the English in the correspondence between Generals Mason and Ross. In Ross' response of 7 September to Mason's letter, the British officer made no allusion to medical aid furnished to members of his command by Beanes, who almost certainly would have mentioned it when he talked personally with the general.[28]

In addition, in an account of the events of August and September, 1814, purportedly given orally by Francis Scott Key himself to his brother-in-law, Roger B. Taney, who was the husband of Key's only sister, Anne, Key said nothing about any professional care extended to the British by Dr. Beanes. Taney recounted Key's version of the rescue mission in an 1856 letter to Key's son-in-law, Charles Howard. The letter was published the following year as a preface to a posthumous volume of Key's poetry. The letter is of particular interest, because of Taney's explanation of why Beanes' captors treated him as a culprit and not as a prisoner of war: "Something must have passed, when the officers were quartered at his house, on the march to Washington, which, in the judgment of General Ross, bound Beanes not to take arms against the English forces until the troops had re-embarked."[29]

What that "something" was—perhaps an oath of good behavior—Taney, Chief Justice of the United States Supreme Court at the time of his letter, did not know. Mrs. William Thornton, wife of the doctor, in her diary entry of 3 September 1814, said the British considered Dr. Beanes' jailing of some of their straggling soldiers as "a breach of his promise of *neutrality*."[30] A century later, Caleb Clarke Magruder, Jr., a descendant through Beanes' sister, Millicent, put forth a similar reading of how the British viewed the conduct of Dr. Beanes. In his address of 15 December 1914 to the Columbia Historical Society of Washington, D.C., Magruder expressed the view that the British commanders construed the friendly offices of Dr. Beanes, when he hosted them in Marlboro, as evidence of Beanes' allegiance to their cause. Accordingly, they interpreted his subsequent actions of instigating the arrest of the British soldiers as tantamount to betrayal.[31] While Magruder did not believe this to be a fair assessment of Beanes' conduct, he did concede that the doctor "carried his policy of diplomacy to such an extreme as to weave his own web of trouble."[32]

What happened with the three Americans following General Ross' decision to free Dr. Beanes, irrespective of whatever kind of web he might have spun, has been told too often, in relation to the origin and writing of "The Star-Spangled Banner," to merit more than a brief word here. The British commanders could hardly permit the Americans to leave the fleet prior to the planned assault by sea and land on Baltimore. The British had often discussed their plans in front of the Americans.[33] On Sunday, 11 September 1814, the day before the attack, Key and Skinner, along with Dr. Beanes, were transferred to their own truce-boat.[34] This small sloop was then anchored with the British transports some eight miles down the Patapsco from Fort McHenry.[35] With the aid of a spyglass the Americans could witness from the packet the British bombardment of the star-shaped fort on 13 and 14 September.[36] Perhaps Dr. Beanes could not since he had no time to collect his spectacles when he had been routed out of bed.[37] It is quite possible, then, as some have plausibly asserted, that the opening line of the anthem was suggested to him by Dr. Beanes, who repeatedly asked his companions whether they could see the huge flag rising over the ramparts of the fort as they waited out the dreadful night.[38]

Following Dr. Beanes' release and return with his rescuers to Baltimore on Friday, 16 September[39] he was able to open up his office to patients once again on the ensuing Monday . He had thirteen years remaining to contemplate the stirring events which involved him in two wars of American independence, one by choice, the other by chance. He passed away at the age of eighty, on 12 October 1828, surviving his wife by six years. Their remains lie in the garden where the British marauders interrupted the party. The garden behind the manor itself was very dear to Dr. Beanes. In his will, witnessed by Francis Scott Key and two others on 24 September 1827, he devised his personal and real property to relatives and friends but specifically reserved "the graveyard in the Garden, which is to be kept up and in complete order by my Executors who are at all times to be permitted to have free access to the same."[40] But with the deaths of the executors and the slow ravages of time, the grave enclosure where William and Sarah Beanes were laid to rest, fell into sad neglect.

Restored grave site and tombs of Dr. William Beanes and his wife, Sarah Hawkins Beanes. Upper Marlboro, Prince George's County, Maryland. Author's photo.

In anticipation of the centennial observance of the birth of the national anthem, the Star-Spangled Banner Society of Prince George's County was formed in 1913 to raise money by private contributions to restore the tombs. The twelve-foot square plot, with its enclosing walls and six columns, surmounted by cannon balls, was completely restored in time for the celebration the next year. Seven decades later, as a result of the damage done by time and the elements, it was again necessary to do major repair and reconstruction. This was undertaken in 1985 by the Prince George's County Committee of the Maryland Historical Trust. A short rededication ceremony was held at the site on 12 November of that year.[41]

Dr. Beanes was also memorialized by being included among ten worthies named to the Hall of Fame of Prince George's County, established in 1975. In an attractive "Directory of Prince Georgians Honored," all are pictured except Dr. Beanes—for whom no likeness is known to exist—and one other. Another Prince Georgian among the portraits is Robert Bowie, who served several terms as governor of Maryland and who was dining in the spring-house of the garden with his host, Dr. Beanes, on that fateful rainy August day in 1814.

At a stage in life when Dr. Beanes could reasonably look forward to a few serene years of gradual retirement, the War of 1812 thrust him into an unexpected chain of events which involved both physical and moral ordeals . Glancing at these events, one cannot cease to marvel how "the ever-whirling wheel of change," in Edmund Spenser's phrase, turned to bring this otherwise obscure and unheroic country doctor a distinctive niche in the annals of his country.

Notes

1. Gen. John Mason to Maj. Gen. Robert Ross, 2 Sept. 1814, in George J. Svejda, *History of the Star-Spangled Banner from 1814 to the Present* (U.S. Dept. of the Interior, National Park Service (Washington, D.C., 1969), p. 61.

2. Lt. Col. Francis S. Key-Smith, "Francis Scott Key and the National Anthem," p. 9, unpublished paper read before the Maryland Historical Society, Baltimore, Md. 14 Oct. 1929.

3. Ibid., p. 10.

4. Caleb Clark Magruder, Jr., "Dr. William Beanes, the Incidental Cause of the Authorship of the Star-Spangled Banner," *Records of the Columbia Historical Society of Washington, D.C., 22 (1919): 209-10.*

5. Francis B. Heitman, *Historical Register of Officers of the Continental Army During the Revolution April 1775 to 1783* (Baltimore, Md.: Genealogical Publishing Co., 1973). Also negative under alternate names of *Banes* and *Beans*, but brother Colmore Beanes, M.D. is listed on p. 94 for service from 25 June to 12 Oct. 1777.

6. William L. Marbury, "The Seizure and Imprisonment of Dr. Beanes," *The Patriotic Marylander*, 1, No. 1 (Sept. 1914): 15.

7. Eugene H. Conner, "William Beanes, M.D. (1749-1829), and 'The Star-Spangled Banner,'" *Journal of the History of Medicine*, 34, No. 2 (1979): 224.

8. Eugene Fauntleroy Cordell, *The Medical Annals of Maryland: 1799-1899* (Baltimore: The Medical and Chirurgical Faculty of the State of Maryland, 1903), p. 22.

9. Ibid., p. 21.

10. Edward Lawrence, "Our National Anthem," *National Magazine*, 14, No. 4 (July 1901): 416.

11. Key-Smith, *Francis Scott Key*, pp. 66-67.

12. [George Robert Gleig], *A Subaltern in America: Comprising His Narrative of the Campaign of the British Army at Baltimore, Washington, &c. &c. During the Late War.* (Philadelphia: E. L. Cary and A. Hart, 1833), p. 46.

13. Key, *Poems*, p. 18.

14. Gleig, pp. 45-46.

15. Key-Smith, *Francis Scott Key*, p. 63.

16. Magruder, "The Incidental Cause of the Authorship of the Star-Spangled Banner," p. 217.

17. W. B. Bryan, "Diary of Mrs. William Thornton. Capture of Washington by the British," *Records of the Columbia Historical Society of Washington, D.C.*, 19 (1916): 179.

18. Gov. Levin Winder to Maj. Gen. Robert Ross, 31 Aug. 1814, in William Marine, *The British Invasion of Maryland, 1812-1815* (Baltimore: Society of the War of 1812 in Maryland, 1913), pp. 189-90.

19. For a complete description of the Battle of Bladensburg, see James Riehl Arnold, "The Battle of Bladensburg," *Records of the Columbia Historical Society of Washington, D. C.*, 37-38 (1937): 145-68; and Walter Lord, *The Dawn's Early Light* (New York, Ny.: W.W. Norton and Co., 1972), pp. 123-43.

20. Key to Randolph, 5 Oct. 1814, in Filby and Howard, p. 160.

21. Jensen, p. 64.

22. Mason to Ross, 2 Sept. 1814, in Svejda, pp. 60-61.

23. For details of this meeting, see Lord, pp. 243-44, and Jensen, p. 64.

24. Ralph J. Robinson, "The Birth of the National Anthem," *Baltimore,* 47, No. 2 (Dec. 1953), p. 65.

25. Arnold, p. 161.

26. Compare Lord, pp. 243-44.

27. Key-Smith, *Francis Scott Key*, p. 67; Weybright, p. 104; and Delaplaine, *Francis Scott Key*, p. 156.

28. Ross to Mason, 7 Sept. 1814, in Robinson, "The Birth of the National Anthem," p. 65.

29. Key, *Poems*, p. 22.

30. Bryan, p. 180.

31. Magruder, "Dr. William Beanes, the Incidental Cause of the Authorship of the Star-Spangled Banner," pp. 220-21.

32. Ibid., p. 221.

33. J. S. Skinner, "Incidents of the War of 1812," *Maryland Historical Magazine*, 32 (Dec. 1937): 347. This statement by Skinner, Key's companion on the mission and an eyewitness to the events on the HM S *Tonnant*, flagship of the British fleet, first appeared in the *Baltimore Patriot and Commercial Gazette*, 29 May 1849.

34. Harold R. Manakee, "Anthem Born in Battle," in Filby and Howard, p. 33.

35. Lord, p. 365.

36. Ibid., p. 292.

37. Stein, p. 18.

38. Ibid., pp. 25-26; Coles, p. 186; and Jay Hubbell, *The South in American Literature, 1607-1900* (Durham, N.C.: Duke University Press, 1954), p. 301.

39. Filby and Howard, p. 45.

40. Maryland State Archives, Hall of Records, Annapolis, Md., Prince George's County (Wills), pp. 432-37 Dr. Beanes with codicils, 18 Oct. 1828. The executors were Dr. Beanes' brother, Colmore, and his friend, John Read Magruder (p. 432).

41. Information on the grave site, which the author visited on 6 June 1987, and on the posthumous honors bestowed upon Dr. Beanes, may be found in the following sources: Magruder, "Dr. William Beanes, the Incidental Cause of the Authorship of the Star-Spangled Banner": 222-24; Magruder, "Dr. William Beanes," *Bulletin of the Medical and Chirurgical Faculty of Maryland*, 7, No. 5 (1914-1915): 69; and *Gravesite of Dr. William Beanes* (Prince George's County Committee, Maryland Historical Trust and Prince George's Heritage, Inc.).

Chapter 5

Chronicle of Contrarieties

Perhaps in all human affairs, revealing paradoxes and contrarieties appear under close examination, but in the case of Francis Scott Key and his noted creation, "The Star-Spangled Banner," ironic contrasts leap out at the attentive observer. As in a many-faceted diamond, these contrarieties reflect light on the man and his works, providing a fresh perspective on both.

One of the ironic circumstances that frequently has been commented upon was that the Battle of New Orleans, the bloodiest engagement of the War of 1812, was fought when the war was officially over. Although the Treaty of Ghent was signed at The Hague on 24 December 1814, news of the official end of the conflict did not reach Washington until 14 February 1815; the carnage at New Orleans took place on January 8th of that year.

Less frequently noted in connection with the Second War of Independence (as contemporaries called it, but which historians later gave the misnomer, "the War of 1812"), is the irony of its being unnecessary. Key and those of like sentiment believed disputes should—and usually could—be settled by peaceful means. But neither Key nor those opposed to the war were aware that the principal cause from the American point of view already had been removed by the time President James Madison signed the proclamation on 18 June 1812, formally committing the United States to the war. This cause was the sweeping British order of council of 16 May 1806, proclaiming a blockade of the European coast and requiring neutral ships to pay fees and obtain British permits to carry non-contraband items through the blockade. The new British foreign secretary, Lord Robert Castlereagh, announced the lifting of the orders of council applicable to the United States on 16 June, two days before the

American president approved the congressional resolution for war! But, unfortunately, because of the long delay of one to two months for communications to cross the Atlantic, the president and the Congress did not learn of the abrogation of the orders until more than a month later. By that time, events had moved beyond the point where the two nations could reach a mutually agreeable settlement of differences.[1]

Despite his abhorrence of war as an instrument of policy and his specific objections to what the Federalists of his time termed "Mr. Madison's war," Key volunteered for active duty in the Maryland Militia in the summer of 1813 and later served in combat at Bladensburg on 24 August 1814.

Less than a month later, he penned the lyric that was to bring him acclaim while living and lasting homage to his memory afterward. In his own day, being hailed at home and in his travels as the author of "The Star-Spangled Banner" was at odds with his essentially reclusive nature and ingrained humility. He held strongly to the Christian belief that one must constantly strive to avoid the sin of Pride and that the only true need for one's good deeds on earth was the sweet rewards to be received in that "new home in the skies." His verses, which contain the just-quoted phrase from "The Worm's Death-Song" and gathered in the small posthumous volume of 1857, contain many warnings against vainglory. For example, in one of the only four poems that their author in his modesty permitted to be printed, "Hymn for the Fourth of July, 1832," Key exhorted the Christian worshipper: "Cast down thy pride, / Thy sin deplore, / And bow before / The crucified."[2]

Another contradiction was Key being, on the one hand, a detester of slavery and, on the other, a slaveholder. Nearing the age of sixty, he declared that there was no one who started out in life with more emotion against slavery than himself.[3] In the hope of alleviating to some degree the lot of manumitted slaves, he helped found the American Colonization Society. To the end of his life he maintained a leading role in championing, against passionate opposition, the society's objective: to transport liberated slaves who so wished to go to free settlements on the west coast of Africa and provide for them and their families once they got there. Given the firmly established practice of the time, with examples set by such revered figures of the Revolution as Patrick Henry, Thomas Jefferson, and George Washington, Key would not have accepted the notion that owning slaves was sinful.

Another ironic aspect of Key's career has drawn more attention in this century than his keeping of slaves. This aspect is the outstanding success he achieved in the fields in which he devoted his best and most sustained efforts—in the law, in the church, in public office as attorney-general for the Federal District, and in his capacity as a diplomat appointed by the president of the United States to help settle domestic disputes. These were all in contrast to his being remembered by posterity almost exclusively for a single deed, the writing of "The Star-Spangled Banner." In the words of his great-grandson and namesake, Francis Scott Key-Smith, "the splendor with which he crowned his name has shone so brightly that it has extinguished the brilliancy of his many other great deeds and signal services."[4]

That these great deeds and signal services were not always given their due in later times was manifested in one case by the fact that, despite strenuous exertions over many years on the part of his admirers, Key was never elected to the United States Hall of Fame for Great Americans. This national shrine, established in 1900 by Chancellor Mitchell MacCracken of New York University and housed at the University Heights campus in the city, elects five leading American men and women every five years to the Hall of Fame. Fifty Americans were chosen in the initial election. The actual selection of nominees is made by one hundred eminent Americans. No one, however, can be considered for election until twenty-five years following his or her death. At least seven men well known to Key have their names inscribed on a bronze tablet inside the Hall—Henry Clay, Rufus Choate, Andrew Jackson, James Madison, John Marshall, James Story, and Daniel Webster.

In 1940 Francis Scott Key was first nominated to the Hall of Fame, but received only eleven votes in the same year Stephen Collins Foster, who wrote many folk songs, was admitted. Key lost again in 1945.[5] The most high-powered campaign for Key was mounted in 1965. The grounds for the nomination took into account Key's varied achievements in addition to his writing of the national anthem. The formal nomination stated the basis on which Key's advocates advanced his candidacy: "Primarily as the author of the National Anthem, also as lawyer, orator, poet, public official, and humanitarian."[6] Notwithstanding strong endorsements by the governor of Maryland, J. Millard Tawes; the Commissioners of the District of Columbia; Daughters of the American Revolution; and other prestigious individuals, Key was decisively defeated.[7]

As with the man, so likewise with his creation. On the one hand there was virulent criticism of the ode; on the other, there was enthusiastic laudation. Criticism has dogged the song most markedly from the time of the Civil War forward to this day, but it may be said to have reached a crescendo in the hotly contested struggle for its adoption by the U.S. Congress and ratification by the president, which was finally achieved on 17 March 1931,[8] 117 years after its composition. Between 1910 and 1929 numerous bills and resolutions to establish the song were introduced in Congress, one or more each year. In all, fifteen Congressmen and two Senators submitted measures one or more times to that purpose, and all failed to pass.[9] To be sure, there were formidable competitors for the distinction of becoming the national song, notably "Hail, Columbia", 1798; "America" or "My Country! 'Tis of Thee," 1832; "Columbia, the Gem of the Ocean," 1843;

"The Battle Hymn of the Republic," 1861; and "America the Beautiful," 1893, 1904. Each had its ardent advocates in and out of Congress. Representative J. Charles Linthicum of Maryland, introduced his first bill, H. R. 11365, to obtain congressional sanction for "The Star-Spangled Banner" on 10 April 1918. After five turn-downs and a lapse of thirteen years, he finally succeeded with his sixth Star-Spangled Banner Bill, H.R. 14, which he had introduced on 15 April 1928, and which passed the Senate on 3 March 1931 and was signed by President Herbert Hoover the same day.

The final wording of the Bill, Public law 8233, 71st Congress, much debated before passage, was simplified to four printed lines and prescribed neither text nor music. It provided only, "That the com-

Congressman J. Charles Linthicum of the 4th Maryland District (1887-1932) sponsored the measure enacted by Congress in 1931 to have "The Star-Spangled Banner" declared the American national anthem. Fort McHenry National Monument and Historic Shrine, Baltimore.

position of the words and music known as "The Star-Spangled Banner" is designated the national anthem of the United States of America."[10]

The reason for the thirteen-year interval between Linthicum's first Banner bill and the last, aside from the other songs in competition, was the vociferous public and legislative opposition to it. Linthicum's opponents in the national legislature were not strong enough to get their own choice selected but collectively they had enough political muscle to keep his bills bottled up in committee. Major credit for Linthicum's eventual triumph must go to Mrs. Reuben Ross Holloway and Mrs. James B. Arthur, president and corresponding secretary, respectively, of the Maryland Society, United States Daughters of 1812, who fought for the bill tooth and nail, and to those they enlisted in their cause.[11] During the long period between Linthicum's first and last bill, persistent strident arguments were aired repeatedly against "The Star-Spangled Banner," not only in Congress but in the press and public forums of the nation at large. Most of the same points of deep displeasure with the official choice continue virtually unabated to this day.

One especially persistent quarrel with the poem, as contrasted, for example, with "My Country! 'Tis of Thee" or "America the Beautiful," has been that it is difficult to memorize, a factor attributable, its critics aver, to its long lines,

Mrs. Reuben Ross Holloway (1862-1940), the moving spirit of the campaign to adopt Key's song as the official anthem. Fort McHenry National Monument and Historic Shrine, Baltimore.

involved rhymes, rather stilted words, and sometimes awkward syntax. One of the classic stories from World War II concerns this complaint. It seems that a soldier coming into an American outpost at night from a patrol of enemy territory was challenged by the guard on duty.

"Who goes there?"

"An American," replied the soldier.

"Then come forward and recite the first verse of "The Star-Spangled Banner," demanded the sentry.

"I can't remember it," was the sheepish reply.

"Pass, American!" quickly responded the guard.

A similar story was told by Hermione Gingold, singer and co-medienne. On the evening of V-Day, 7 May 1945, the stage performers in England had to sing all the Allies' national anthems and learn the words. Some American soldiers in the audience called out, "Don't bother to learn the words to 'The Star-Spangled Banner.' We'll be sitting right here in the first row. We'll sing them for you." Years later Ms. Gingold wryly recalled: "Well, they got as far as the first line and then they didn't know the words after that. It was really awful."[12]

Another instance of the song being difficult to recall was demonstrated to the public on 25 May 1965, during the world heavyweight fight between Cassius Clay and Sonny Liston at Lewiston, Maine. Just prior to the one-minute bout in which Clay knocked out Liston, Robert J. Goulet, singing star of stage and television, began singing the national anthem but had to stop abruptly when he forgot the words and had to consult his crib in full camera view. Both gaffes were viewed on closed circuit screens in various theaters across the country, including the Capitol Theater in New York City, where a sellout crowd of 1,500 watched.[13]

Not only is "The Star-Spangled Banner" hard to commit to memory but its detractors frequently allege that it is difficult to sing properly, which makes it unsuitable to be the nation's signal song. At least as early as the Civil War period, in a book entitled *National Hymns: How They are Written and How They are Not Written*, Richard Grant White, after conceding that the song had been growing in popularity in the loyal states from the beginning of the secession movement and was being played continually by military and orchestral bands and often sung at concerts and private musical gatherings, declared:

But as a patriotic song for the people at large, as the
National Hymn, it was found to be almost useless. The
range of the air, an octave and a half, places it out of
the compass of ordinary voices; and no change that has
been made in it has succeeded in obviating this para-
mount objection, without depriving the music of that
characteristic spirit which is given by its quick ascent
through such an extended range of notes.[14]

Two wars later, Lucy Monroe, soprano of the Metropolitan
Opera, who attained fame for singing "The Star-Spangled Banner"
five thousand times during World War II, asserted that the music is
difficult for an untrained voice, that almost all singers are unable to
handle the high notes and usually merely hum that part or stop singing for a few measures.[15]

A more recent complaint came from a contributor to the nationally syndicated column of the contemporary Miss Lonely Hearts,
Ann Landers. In the April 4, 1985 issue of the *Chicago Sun-Times*,
the contributor appealed to the columnist in these words regarding
the anthem:

I believe it should be discarded, and in its place we
should adopt "America the Beautiful."

To begin with, "The Star-Spangled Banner" has a
range that is virtually impossible for the average person
to manage. The word "gleaming" is almost inaudible
because it is so far down in the register. "And the
rockets' red glare" is difficult to reach because it is so
high. Wherever our national anthem is sung most
people have to change an octave. Please crusade for
this change, Ann.[16]

The columnist, in response, gave short shrift to this plea:
"You've made some valid points, but I am still recovering from a
sex survey and cannot take on anything more at this time."

Both complaints about the Banner song's being difficult to learn
by heart and difficult to sing were summed up in an epigram by a
writer in the *New York Herald Tribune* who asserted that Key was
"the forgotten man who wrote the words that nobody can remember,
to the tune nobody can sing, and hence became famous as the author
of the national anthem."[17]

Still another argument about "The Star-Spangled Banner" focused on the tune itself. Critics pointed out that the song derived its air from an English ballad, rendering the American song inappropriate as an expression of the national voice. This charge was at its height during the Prohibition Era of the 1920s and was a major plank in the platform of those who sought strenuously to block passage of bills in Congress to legalize Key's lyric as America's No. 1 song. This whole issue merits attention because the song is still derogated because of its allegedly disreputable origin.

It is true that the melody to which Key consciously or subconsciously adapted the meter, rhyme, and word arrangement parallels "Anacreon in Heaven." This lyric, named after Anacreon, a sixth century, B.C., Greek poet, who celebrated in his verses the twin joys of love and wine, was the constitutional song of the Anacreontic Society, a London club that met regularly at the Crown and Anchor tavern in the Strand from 1777 until its dissolution at the end of 1792. Ralph Tomlinson, first president of the Society, wrote the words to the "Anacreontic Song" and probably John Stafford Smith set them to music.[18] The Anacreontic Society, meeting at the then well-known English public house was a respectable, even prestigious, social club. A musician, William T. Parke, who played regularly at the Society beginning in 1786, wrote in his memoirs that to become a member "noblemen and gentlemen would wait a year for a vacancy."[19]

Although the "Anacreontic Song" did allude to Venus and Bacchus in its choral couplets, the opponents of the American anthem were off the mark when they implied that the original song from which the Banner tune was borrowed was coarse or indecent. Reading the English lyric carefully, one searches in vain for the Bacchanalian spirit or licentious ribaldry attributed to it. Like the American song that imitated the meter, verse arrangement, and the melody of its musical predecessor, each stanza of "Anacreon" had a chorus in couplets, which for the six stanzas was a slight variant of the sentiment expressed in the last:

> And long may the sons of Anacreon entwine
> The myrtle of Venus with Bacchus' vine.[20]

The tune of "Anacreon" was immensely popular and spread quickly across the Atlantic. The Anacreontic model thoroughly permeated the new republic in Key's time. Richard Hill, then a reference librarian in the music division of the Library of Congress, in an

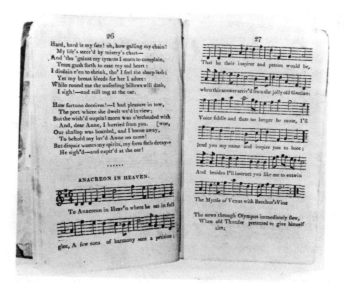

The English social club melody, "Anacreon In Heaven" as published in the "Baltimore Musical Miscellany" in 1804. Maryland Historical Society, Baltimore.

essay of 1951, reported that no less than eighty-five parodies of the "Anacreontic Song" were published in America from 1785 to 1820.[21] In the essay Hill gave the first two lines of each parody that he found in his search of newspapers, magazines, and books. Of the eighty-five, twenty-six came before "When the Warrior Returns from the Battle Afar," Key's dress rehearsal for "The Star-Spangled Banner,"[22] which also has several phrases similar to those used in his later anthem, such as the line from the third stanza, "By the light of the star-spangled flag of our nation." Lyrics patterned after "To Anacreon," most with patriotic themes, proliferated in the States following the appearance of the popular ballad, "Adams and Liberty," written by Robert Treat Paine in 1798 for a Fourth of July celebration. Prior to "The Star-Spangled Banner," there were at least sixty-eight parodies in America.[23] Key's song in its first-known printing as a broadside under the title, "Defence of Fort McHenry," had the notation, "Tune—Anacreon in Heaven" at the bottom of fourteen explanatory lines.[24]

Since the words were precisely suited to the popular melody, or, as some would have it, Key made up a text to fit an extant tune,[25] people would have had little or no difficulty following the tune. Moreover, Key himself quite possibly joined in the singing of his

"When the Warrior Returns"[26] at a dinner on 30 November 1805. The dinner was held in Georgetown to celebrate the triumphant return of naval heroes Stephen Decatur and Charles Stevens from the war in Tripoli against the Barbary Coast pirates the previous year.[27]

Thus, by the time Key put his words to the harmony of "Anacreon," the tune was so thoroughly familiar to him and to other Americans that its origin as a club song from across the water was most likely not known to him or to its other numerous imitators in America; even if it was, that fact would hardly have given them pause. In view of Key's and his compatriots' relative indifference to the British origin of the tune—if indeed they were even aware of it—at a time when tension between the two English-speaking countries ran high because of the war, it is ironic that twentieth-century patriots railed against "The Star-Spangled Banner" on the very ground of its British and public house origins. Of course, this later opposition was part of the fight to block passage of congressional bills to legalize Key's song. Yet the accusations appeared sincere; something more needs to be said on the bitter fight to prevent it from becoming the national anthem.

According to Joseph Muller in his *Bibliography* of 1935, "The Star-Spangled Banner" held first place in the ranks of national songs during the Civil War, the Spanish-American War, and World War II, [28] among such formidable rivals as "America," the "Battle Hymn of the Republic," and "America, the Beautiful." Moreover, by 1916 the Armed Forces regarded it as the official national anthem. Despite this éclat, Ms. Kitty Cheatham started an organized and well-financed campaign in 1918 to forestall the passage of any Banner bill. Another leader in the acrimonious fight against recognition was Ms. Augusta E. Stetson, who attracted much attention by publishing in prominent newspapers advertisements attacking Key's song. Both of these doughty ladies and many others assailed "The Star-Spangled Banner" as America's premier song on the basis of its objectionable origin, drawing no distinction between lyric and music. Stetson, for example, in advertisements in the *New York Tribune* on 11 June 1922, and in the *Baltimore Sun* and *The Washington Post* on 13 June of that same year, strongly urged Americans to repudiate Key's ode because, in her opinion, it was "a poem born of intense hatred of Great Britain and wedded to a barroom ballad composed by a foreigner."[29] The second part of her charge has just been taken up. Stetson's implication that the Banner poem was

Anglophobic in its sentiments became a keynote of the campaign against passage of Linthicum's measure and was to be repeated by its antagonists almost ad infinitum. In addition, Cheatham, in a long and impassioned letter to President Herbert Hoover, dated 24 January 1930, highlighted the accusation in a last-ditch effort to head off passage of the bill. She declared that " 'The Star-Spangled Banner' " is fundamentally a song of resentment against our natural brother, Great Britain."[30]

Those who, like Stetson and Cheatham, railed against Key's lyric because it cast aspersions upon members of the British Expeditionary Force in the War of 1812 were on stronger ground than those who argued against it mainly because of its tavern associations. The resentment focused, of course, on the third stanza:

And where are the foes who so vauntingly swore
    That the havoc of war, and the battle's confusion,
A home and a country should leave us no more:
Their blood has washed out their foul footsteps'
    pollution;
No refuge could save the hireling and slave
From the terror of flight, or the gloom of the grave;
And the Star-Spangled Banner in triumph doth wave
O'er the land of the free and the home of the brave![31]

This stanza clearly speaks of vengeance against the British foes who had boasted that they would devastate American cities but who were now deservingly dead or in flight. The sentiment expressed is uncharacteristic of its author. Ordinarily, Key's deeply ingrained Christian doctrines of charity, mercy, and forgiveness would have precluded such bitter expression. But this vindictive outburst may be better understood if one recalls the anguish that he must have lived through on that night, when he watched with horror and suspense the furious bombardment of Fort McHenry from the truce-boat outside Baltimore harbor.[32] He was highly indignant, moreover, about the fact that many of Major General Robert Ross' invading force of 4,000 were mercenary soldiers from countries other than the British Isles.

Key's great-grandson, Francis Scott Key-Smith, included explanations such as these for the third stanza in an unpublished paper that he read before the Maryland Historical Society in Baltimore on 14 October 1929. Key-Smith, an authority on the life and times of his distinguished forebear and the author of a short biography of him, apparently felt the need to answer the critics who vented their spleen against both the author and the stanza when the fate of the prospective national anthem was at a critical stage in Congress. Key-Smith recalled in his remarks to the Historical Society that Francis Scott Key had written to his close friend, John Randolph, that General Ross had boasted he would take Baltimore and make it his winter quarters even if it rained militia. Key-Smith went on to point out that the reference to "Hireling" and "Slave" pertained to the large number of troops engaged in the combined sea and land attack against Baltimore who were hired soldiers and "not British subjects fighting for patriotic reasons."[33] Long after the issue was moot, the matter of the third stanza seemed to have continued to be a sensitive one to Key-Smith. Indeed, at the age of seventy-six—two years before his death on 25 February 1951—when he was proposing to speak again before the Maryland Historical Society on his great-grandfather's poetry, he was interview by a reporter for the *Baltimore Sun*. The journalist said Key-Smith quoted the third stanza in a trembling voice. Key-Smith told the reporter that leaving out that verse made the poem incomplete.

Technically, the third stanza still belongs in the anthem because Congress has never mandated a standard version of either the text or the music. However, years before the issue of which was to be the official song of the nation was up before Congress and the people, the common understanding was that the third stanza was to be left out. The proceedings of the influential National Education Association's annual general meeting held in 1912 in Milwaukee eliminated stanza three of the poem. At this meeting the NEA suggested a "current official version" that omitted this stanza.[34] From that time on, the verse never appeared in songbooks and seldom in print elsewhere. Furthermore, it became the custom to sing only the opening and sometimes the closing fourth stanza at ceremonial occasions, sporting events, and other public assemblies.

Consequently, two of the main issues chosen by opponents to block the Star-Spangled bills in Congress were in essence already moot. The hullabaloo against Key's penultimate stanza served as little more than rhetorical ammunition in the fierce and prolonged fight to determine which song was to become the national anthem. The strident cries of indignation against the adoption of "The Star-Spangled Banner" as America's premier song because its air originally had been that of the signal song of the English tavern club and therefore "un-American" proved equally unconvincing in the end.

Overall, despite the hue and cry, supporters of Key's lyric have praised it highly for its lofty tone and its true patriotic spirit. They even invite attention to the fact that in 1904 the Italian composer, Giacomo Puccini, deemed its music good enough for the overture of his opera, *Madame Butterfly*. They also point out that it is the only national anthem that is dedicated to its country's flag. What its composer regarded at the time of its hasty composition as an occasional piece dealing with a single stirring event in his country's history—which he happened to be on the scene to witness—is likely to remain the official anthem of the republic. In addition, its author, despite his rejection of worldly renown, became renowned around the world anyway.

Notes

1. Bruce Catton and William B. Catton, *The Bold and Magnificent Dream: America's Founding Years*, 1492-1815 (Garden City, N.Y.: Doubleday and Co., 1978), pp. 451,461.
2. Key, *Poems*, p. 97.
3. Delaplaine, *Francis Scott Key*, p. 191.
4. Key-Smith, *Francis Scott Key*, p. 6.
5. Browne, *The Story of Our National Ballads,* p. 54.
6. Edward S. Delaplaine, *John Philip Sousa and the National Anthem* (Frederick, Md.: Great Southern Press, 1983), p. 2.
7. Ibid.
8. Quasi-official status was conferred upon "The Star-Spangled Banner," prior to its adoption by Congress. In 1889 the Secretary of the Navy ordered the song played on naval vessels at morning and evening colors; in 1903 for "special occasions" in both the Army and Navy, officers and men were ordered to stand at attention whenever and wherever the song was rendered; and one year prior to American entry into World War I, President Woodrow Wilson, by Executive Order, proclaimed the Banner song the national anthem, but this order did not apply when his term ended (Browne, p. 56).
9. The history of repetitive resolutions and acts in Congress during this interval in the effort to legalize "The Star-Spangled Banner" is detailed in Svejda, pp. 342-84. An account of the proceedings of the last day of the last session of the 71st Congress, when the fate of the Star-Spangled bill was hanging in the balance, is given in Delaplaine, *John Philip Sousa and the National Anthem*, pp. 81-83.
10. For a facsimile of original bill declaring "The Star-Spangled Banner"

the national anthem, see Joseph Muller, comp., *The Star-Spangled Banner Words and Music Issued Between 1814-1864: An Annotated Bibliographic List* (New York: G. G. Baker and Co., Inc., 1935), p. 37.

11. *The New York Times* obituary of Mrs. Holloway (1870-1940) credited her outstanding achievement among the many public causes that she espoused in her lifetime her spearheading the fight for the adoption by Congress of "The Star-Spangled Banner" as the leading song of the nation (*The New York Times*, 1 Dec. 1940, p. 62, col. 3).

12. Charles Braun, "Let's Waive 'The Star-Spangled Banner,'" *Fact*, 2, No. 1 (Jan.-Feb. 1965): 13.

13. Svejda, pp. 444-45.

14. Richard Grant White, *National Hymns: How They Are Written and How They Are Not Written* (New York: Rudd and Carleton, 1861), pp. 17-18.

15. Braun, p. 6.

16. "Ann Landers," *Chicago Sun-Times*, 4 April 1985, p. 72.

17. Edward S. Delaplaine, *Maryland in Law and History* (New York: Vantage Press, 1964), p. 45, reprinted from *Francis Scott Key and the National Anthem* (Washington, D.C.: Wilson Epson Press, 1947), p. 3.

18. Oscar George Theodore Sonneck, comp., *Report on "The Star-Spangled Banner" "Hail Columbia" "Yankee Doodle"* (Washington, D.C.: Govt. Printing Office, 1909), pp. 20-21.

19. William Lichtenwanger, "The Music of 'The Star-Spangled Banner' from Ludgate to Capitol Hill," *Library of Congress Quarterly Journal*, 34, No. 3 (July 1977): 142.

20. Sonneck, p. 21.

21. Richard Hill, "The Melody of the 'The Star-Spangled Banner' in the United States before 1820," in *Essays Honoring Lawrence C. Wroth*, ed. Frederick R. Goff (Portland, Me., 1954): 178.

22. Ibid., p. 168.

23. Ibid., p. 175.

24. Filby and Howard, Plate 21, p. 64.

25. Lichtenwanger, p. 147.

26. Hill, pp. 168-69.

27. Weybright, pp. 147-48.

28. Muller, p. 36.

29. Svejda, p. 360.

30. Copy, Library of Congress, Music Library.

31. Key, *Poems*, pp. 32-33.

32. Key-Smith, "Fort McHenry and the 'Star-Spangled Banner'": 18-19.

33. Key-Smith, "Francis Scott Key and the National Anthem": 24.

34. John T. Silkett, *Francis Scott Key and the History of the Star-Spangled Banner* (Washington, D.C.: Vintage American Publishing Co., 1978), p. 36.

Chapter 6

Homage of the Heart:
Six Statuary Monuments

On Flag Day in 1922, a huge statue dedicated to the memory of Francis Scott Key was unveiled on the front lawn of Fort McHenry in Baltimore. For the ceremony President Warren G. Harding lent his presence to render his tribute. One of the many fine things he said of Key during the dedication exercises was: "No pursuit of fame set his soul ablaze."[1]

The Reverend John T. Brooke, who knew Key well as his parishioner in Georgetown for several years, spoke of Key in a similar vein when on 29 January 1843, he delivered the memorial sermon at Christ's Church in Cincinnati, following Key's death from pneumonia on 11 January. In his eulogy the rector emphasized Key's self-effacing nature. He told the congregation that the time other professionals gave to secular study, "with an eye to the heights of a more worldly ambition," Key spent in sacred reading or in acts of benevolence and charity to others.[2]

Many of Key's colleagues and friends shared the assessment of Key's character as being modest and unassuming . Accordingly, it is paradoxical that after his passing—when he was forever beyond the temptations of mortal vainglory—more honors have been heaped upon his memory than for any other writers of patriotic songs. Still another impressive memorial to him recently was completed at Thirty-fourth and M Streets, N.W., in his adoptive city of Washington, D.C., where he lived with his family and practiced law from about 1805 to the end of his life.

This is the latest of six major remembrances to Key. It owes its existence to the Francis Scott Key Park Foundation, Inc., composed of professionals from both the public and private sectors. Enabling legislation by the Federal Government, Public Law 99-534, was sponsored in Congress by Representative Mary Rose Oakar (D-Ohio), and Senator Frank Murkowski (R-Alaska). Signed by President Ronald W. Reagan on 27 October 1986, it authorized the Foundation "to erect a memorial on public grounds in the District of Columbia in honor and in commemoration of Francis Scott Key, the author of the words to 'The Star-Spangled Banner,' our National Anthem." The entire project was to be at no cost to the government.

By mid-1990, the Foundation had raised about half of its projected goal of one million dollars.[3] Owing to delays caused by the need to get official clearances from the District of Columbia, the Commission of Fine Arts, the National Capital Planning Commission, the National Memorial Commission, and the National Park Service, as well as shortfalls in funding from voluntary contributions from individuals and organizations, actual site preparation did not begin until the spring of 1989. But work then proceeded so quickly that the Foundation was able to hold a celebration on the site to observe the 175th anniversary of the birth of the national ode on 24 September 1989. On the afternoon of that bright Sunday, a reduced replica of the flag of 1814, with its fifteen stars and fifteen stripes, was first raised to conclude the colorful ceremony.

The Francis Scott Key Park, Georgetown, Washington, D.C. looking South toward Virginia. The park sits just east of the Francis Scott Key Bridge, very close to where Key lived when he wrote the national anthem. Francis Scott Key Foundation.

Four years later, on another halcyon day in the capital, Tuesday, 14 September 1993, the park, completed and now grandly designated the Francis Scott Key Park-The Star-Spangled Banner Monument, was dedicated with elaborate fanfare—a parade, band-playing, speeches and, of course, renditions of the National Anthem. "The Star-Spangled Banner" was sung by Dionne Warwick at St. John's Episcopal Church, which Key helped found in 1817; and by Sandi Patti as the finale of the dedication at the site itself, appropriately only a few blocks east of Key's former mansion on M Street.

During the dedication, Washington, D.C. Mayor, Sharon Pratt Kelly, presented the park to the National Park Service for maintenance in perpetuity. The transfer was acknowledged by Robert Stanton, National Capital Region Director.

The penultimate event of the dedication was, fittingly, the ceremonious raising of Old Glory. The cord was drawn by an actor, Alan Gephardt, playing the role of Francis Scott Key and dressed in the colorful uniform of an officer in the Maryland Militia, circa 1814, which Key had been. The huge crowd in attendance breathed a sigh of relief when the ensign rose smoothly to the top of the staff, there set to wave day and night ever after.

The park was designed by Oehme, van Sweden and Associates, specialists in the planning of urban parks. Its centerpiece is a pergola, set with plain limestone columns around a circular brownstone platform. On the platform just south of the pergola where it opens up stands a life-sized bronze bust of Francis Scott Key, mounted on a granite pedestal, some seven feet high. The sculpture, executed by Betty Mailhouse Dunston, can be seen from everywhere in the memorial. Key's upper body faces east but his head and neck shift slightly as if, commented James van Sweden of the designing firm, Key were turning to look once more at the cherished flag of his country.

Aside from its memorial features, the park is planned to accommodate various activities. A bicycle path trails up the hillside from the Chesapeake and Ohio Canal. The main walkway of the area lies close to the M Street sidewalk, luring pedestrians on a pleasant detour or to a resting bench a short distance from the city's hustle and bustle. The walkway in turn connects with a brownstone stairway to Thirty-first Street, where it declines steeply to the Old Mule Bridge across the Canal.

The new park is a welcome replacement for the refuse-littered derelict of the preceding seventy years. It tastefully honors the com-

The bronze bust of Key sculpted by Betty Mailhouse Dunston. It is visible from almost every view in the Francis Scott Key Park, Georgetown. Francis Scott Key Park Foundation, Washington, D.C.

poser of the official national lyric in a location close to where he lived when he wrote the song. As a public-spirited citizen, Key would doubtless have approved the commitment of the long-neglected half acre to public use and pleasure.

The memorial park is a fitting crown to the efforts of "Randy" Roffman, who was largely responsible in 1982 for encouraging development of the honorary park to Key; is a recompense for the decade-long labors of the Francis Scott Key Foundation, Incorporated, headed in turn by Norman L. Larsen and Jonda McFarlane, with the untiring help of members of their Board of Directors;* and

---

*See Appendix for the full roster of the Foundation.

Key bust in the park.

is a gratification to the Foundation's many financial supporters who raised $3.7 million dollars in all over the years. This huge sum came from individual contributors across the nation, from founding sponsors (Coca-Cola USA, Kmart Corporation, The Thomas J. Lipton Company, McDonald's Corporation), from donors (Martin Marietta Corporation, J.W. Marriott Corporation, Phillip Morris companies, National Geographic Society) and from other firms and institutions.

The actuality of at long last having a monument to Key in Washington, D.C., comparable in visibility to those existing elsewhere in the nation should go a long way toward silencing a frequently voiced grievance that a distinguished American hero has yet to be appropriately honored in our nation's capital.[4] Of the more than five hundred statues in the city, for example, not one was of its illustrious resident who had been a leading member of the bar, public servant, and lay church official during the first half of the nineteenth century.

The new initiative by the Francis Scott Key Park Foundation, Inc., incorporated in the Federal District on 13 January 1983, was the first in Washington or elsewhere in nearly seven decades to recognize in a major way Key's signal contribution to the nation. The completed construction of a park featuring a portrait sculpture of Key near a main gateway to the seat of the national government invites attention to those five imposing statements in stone and bronze that exist outside the capital. The fact that the man honored by them probably would not have wanted them does not affect the consideration they merit both for their intrinsic interest and for their significance as part of our republic's heritage. These five monuments are the statue of Key in Golden Gate Park, San Francisco (1888); the statue of him at his final burial site at Mt. Olivet Cemetery in Frederick, Maryland (1898); the Marburg statue of Key at Eutaw Place in Baltimore, Maryland (1911); the marker at Terra Rubra, Key's birthplace near Keysville, Maryland (1915); and the Orpheus statue at Fort McHenry National Monument and Historic Shrine, Baltimore, Maryland (1922).

Although the first statue of Key, the huge edifice in Golden Gate Park, has been twice removed before being placed in its present location on a knoll at the entrance to the park near the Music Concourse, it presents to the visitor the same imposing spectacle as it did when it was dedicated on the Fourth of July, 1888. Damaged by the 1908 earthquake, it was restored and moved westward in 1909.

The Golden Gate Park monument to Key in San Francisco, California. It was the first monument erected to the memory of Key. Author's photo.

In 1968 it was dismantled and stored to make room for a new science building, but reassembled in time for its rededication on Flag Day of the country's Bicentennial Year.[5]

At the initial dedication, according to the San Francisco *Evening Bulletin* of 5 July 1888, ten thousand people witnessed the ceremonies in the park. The multitude cheered, reported the *Bulletin*, when the national colors enveloping the bronze figure of Francis Scott Key were swept away by the poet's great-grandchildren, Gertrude Cutts and Temple Grayson.[6] The unveiled statue depicted a handsome young man sitting in a baroque bell-tower setting, his face registering the calm of deep concentration.

The monument itself, gift of philanthropist James Lick, who left $60,000 in his will for its construction,[7] was executed in Italy by the then well-known sculptor, William Westmore Story, and shipped to California.[8] Designed in the grand manner of nineteenth-century European sculptures, the elaborate work calls for a brief description. The life-sized figure of Key is supported by a pedestal of travertine. Upon its panels are engraved the four stanzas of the patriotic hymn, a nine-line dedication, and a lyre entwined with oak and olive. Above the figure rises a canopy of stone upheld by four Corinthian columns with carved capitals. Upon these capitals stand four bronze eagles, and over each arch hangs a festoon of flowers held up by a buffalo head. Crowning the dome rises the allegorical form of America, bearing the national ensign and a sheathed sword.

At the 1888 ceremonies, General W. H. Barnes, who presented the statue to the city of San Francisco on behalf of the trustees, mentioned that some years before, there was an effort in Key's native state of Maryland to erect a monument in his honor.[9] The site decided on was in Frederick, where Key lived and conducted law practice from 1801 to 1805, but the venture, suggested first in 1876 by General Edward Shriver,[10] barely got off the ground because of lack of funds.

Several years were to pass before a young editor of *The News* in Frederick, Folger McKinsey, revived the movement. Spurred by the knowledge that a statue of Key had been erected in California (set in place in 1887), the group managed to raise $1,000 from 1890 to 1894, but this sum was too small for practical purposes since they figured they needed at least $15,000 to build a suitable memorial. They decided to organize on a larger scale and to proceed more vigorously. Accordingly, McKinsey and his friends formed the Francis Scott Key Monument Association and launched a nationwide campaign to raise money for the project. Eventually they raised over $25,000. Much of this sum came from dimes and dollars sent in by individuals, especially schoolchildren, from all over the country. The figure also included an appropriation of $5,000 from the State of Maryland.[11]

In 1897 the commission to design and construct the monument was awarded to Alexander Doyle, a prominent sculptor from New York City. Doyle took into his employ a recently arrived twenty-seven-year-old Italian, Pompeo Coppini. The contribution of Coppini to the design and execution of the monument was not known to the public until the 1950s because he always gave credit to Doyle. But a half century after the work was completed Coppini wrote a letter in August, 1953 to Edward S. Delaplaine, who had published a biography of Key in 1937, acknowledging that he had done both the design and the sculpture.[12]

That Coppini, who had been rigorously trained as a sculptor in his native Italy, did a creditable job was recognized early when a critic, writing in the December 1898 issue of *Munsey's Magazine* praised the work as being "a simple, graceful, and poetic monument; a fit memorial for the poet of patriotism."[13]

This favorable assessment is frequently echoed by visitors who come by the thousands each year to view the towering figure that greets them as they enter Mt. Olivet Cemetery, located at the southern entrance to Frederick.

The monument merits description in some detail since it is undoubtedly the most renowned memorial to Key, aside from the national ode itself. The sculpture portrays Key standing as he might have stood on that second Wednesday of September, 1814, when "by the dawn's early light" he glimpsed through the mist the flag of his country still waving aloft over the ramparts of Fort McHenry. His attitude is one of exaltation; with his right arm he indicates the flag, and with the left doffs his hat in salute to it.

At the base of the granite pedestal is a group of three allegorical figures in bronze. The central one is that of the goddess Columbia. Above the goddess' waist is a broad band ornamented around the lower border with raised stars and in the center with a shield and

The monument to Key at the Mt. Olivet Cemetery, Frederick, Maryland during the re-dedication ceremony on Jume 9, 1987. Frederick News-Post, Frederick, Maryland.

eagle. The right arm grasps the stars and stripes, the staff of which is topped by a spread eagle. On the left of Columbia or Liberty stands a youth, his right hand resting on a sword. On her right is a child, holding a lyre. The seal of Maryland is carved on the base beneath the group. At the back of the monument is a tablet containing the text of "The Star-Spangled Banner," which Coppini first modeled in clay, letter by letter, before he was able to read any English.[14]

When the city of Frederick dedicated the monument with grand pomp on 9 August 1898, the speaker of the day was Henry Watterson, a Kentucky journalist widely known for his eloquence. In the course of his long tribute, he reminded his audience that in a crypt beneath the statue lay the mortal remains of Francis Scott Key and those of his wife, Mary.[15]

Full-dress rededications of the Mt. Olivet monument were held in 1914 and 1969, respectively, to mark the centennial and sesquicentennial of the writing of the national song, but the most elaborate rededication took place on Sunday, 7 June 1967, to celebrate the recent restoration of the monument. Two years earlier it had been dismantled and shipped to the Cincinnati, Ohio, workshop of Eleftherios Karkadoulias for a complete renovation at a cost of some $50,000, including funds for future upkeep.[16] The money was raised through private donations, grants from the city of Frederick, the Cemetery Board, and the Francis Scott Key Memorial Foundation. Key's descendants, Francis Scott Key, Sr., and Francis Scott Key, Jr., unveiled the renewed statue. The guest speaker was U.S. Representative Beverly Byron of Maryland. The general chairpersons of the Key Rededication Committee, which planned and arranged the event, were Mrs. Elizabeth B. Delaplaine and Mr. H. Thomas Summers. Alongside Key's monument and last resting place there is a replica of the flag that his song celebrated; the flag is never lowered.

The next statue erected to commemorate Key stands in a small park at Eutaw Place and Lanvale Street in Baltimore. Less grand than the one at Mt. Olivet Cemetery, it is not nearly as well known. Indeed, many Baltimoreans are unaware of its existence. This bronze and granite structure was the gift of Charles L. Marburg, who left $25,000 in his will for its construction. The sculptor was Jean M. A. Mercie of France.[17]

The thirty-foot monument depicts Key standing in an open boat. The boat rests in a fountain basin, on either side of which are

The Marburg Memorial to Key at Eutaw Place, Baltimore, Maryland. Author's photo.

gilt bronze scenes of Fort McHenry. The young Georgetown poet-lawyer appears to be addressing the symbolic figure of Columbia, who holds aloft the gilded national banner. When the statue was unveiled on 15 May 1911, Key's right hand grasped a torch to illuminate the flag, but the torch has since disappeared, along with part of one oar. With his left hand, the suppliant offers to the spirit of America his poem, destined to become the national anthem. The boat itself, one should note parenthetically, lacks historicity since the flag-of-truce vessel for Key and John S. Skinner, who accompanied him in his mission to rescue Dr. William Beanes from the British, was large enough to hold more than thirteen.[18] In Mercie's sculpture, a single barefoot sailor plies the oars in the open boat. Many Baltimore youngsters must have been unable to resist climbing into the vessel. One Baltimorean wrote in 1951 that while the statue did not rate high as a work of art, it was nevertheless an unending delight to little boys.[19]

At the dedication of the Marburg Memorial, Key's granddaughter, Mrs. William Gilmore, pulled off an American flag that had been draped over the figure of Key. Maryland Supreme Court judge, W. Stuart Symington, Jr., delivered the principal address.[20]

Visitors will have to go somewhat out of their way if they wish to glimpse the next monument to be erected. It marks Key's birthplace at Terra Rubra in north central Maryland, not far from the Pennsylvania border. Terra Rubra lies off Route 194, one and one-half miles on the Keysville-Bruceville Road. Terra Rubra, the name generally given to the patriarchal manor and surrounding grounds where Key and his only sibling, Anne, were born and spent their childhood, is in one way the most appropriate place for a memorial to him because it remained a place for him to come home to throughout his life. In his 1911 biography, Key's great-grandson, Francis Scott Key-Smith, sketched a charming word picture of Key and his sister's growing up at Pipe Creek, as Key himself preferred to call the ancestral estate of nearly 3,000 acres, with its creek and fertile valleys skirted by tall, wooded mountain ranges.[21] Late in life, Key recalled in a poem, "To My Sister," the pastoral ambiance of the broad acres that surrounded the mansion.[22] Still in apparent good health, he made his last visit to Terra Rubra in December of 1842. Upon his death the next year, his widow sold the Pipe Creek house, which stood until a storm blew part of it down in 1858.[23] It was replaced the next year by the present building, a farmhouse typical of the region.

In front of this mid-nineteenth century structure now is a tall, white marble marker, with a six-line inscription on its face giving

The 1915 monument at Terra Rubra, Keysville, Maryland, marks the site of Key's birthplace. The building shown is a later farmhouse on the site. Carroll County Historical Society, Westminster, Maryland.

Key's name and date of birth,[24] the date of the dedication, 12 June 1915, and the monument's donors—the Patriotic Order of America and the Pupils of the Public Schools. Above the inscription ripples his country's flag in bas-relief.

The next monument built in tribute to Key—the statue of Orpheus at Fort McHenry—has been controversial since its gala dedication on Flag Day of 1922. Congress appropriated $75,000 in July of 1914 for this monument.[25] On 16 May 1916, Charles H. Niehaus was chosen from a field of thirty-four applicants by the Fine Arts Commission of the Federal Government to be the winner of the award to design and build the edifice, but construction was delayed by the war.[26]

At the monument's dedication, President Harding, addressed the audience at length on the service rendered to his country by the author of the then-unofficial national hymn. Catherine Broening, daughter of the Mayor of Baltimore and Marie Niehaus, daughter of the sculptor, rather than any of the numerous available descendants of the honoree, were chosen to unveil the immense bronze figure of Orpheus.[27]

Statue of Orpheus at Fort McHenry National Monument and Historic Shrine, Baltimore. A profile bust of Key is at the base of the statue. Author's photo.

In its commanding location on the entrance road to Fort McHenry, the colossal statue dominates the surrounding scene. Its location has evoked the indignation of some detractors. They claim its lofty prominence distracts viewers from the replica of the huge flag of 1814,[28] which rises on its ninety-six foot staff just beyond the sally port in the parade area of the partly reconstructed fort.

The Orpheus monument consists of a fifteen-foot high circular base of white marble, ornamented with a frieze in low relief. The frieze begins with a medallion portrait of Key. On either side of the medallion are patriotic insignia, and the drum is encircled with a procession of the Muses of Graeco-Roman mythology. Above the circular pedestal stands a twenty-two foot high nude figure of Orpheus in bronze, shown playing on a five-stringed tortoise-shell lyre.

Serious and persistent criticism has focused on the figure of Orpheus. When visitors to the fort first catch sight of the statue, many reportedly ask, "Who is that Indian?" and "Why is he at Fort McHenry?"[29] The first question may come from the fact that Orpheus is nude; some seem to be offended by this. He is nude because the neoclassical sculptor, Niehaus, claimed that it was impossible to do this kind of a heroic figure clothed.[30]

The second inquiry might question the connection between the author of the patriotic song and the legendary musician. Key could easily have answered the question, knowing Orpheus from his classical studies as "the sweetest singer of antiquity." He would have recalled from Ovid's *Metamorphoses* how Orpheus, by touching his lyre and singing, had persuaded the hitherto implacable rulers of Hades to let him bring back his beloved wife Eurydice from the dark realms of the dead. At the same time, Key, with his ingrained modesty, would have deprecated the aptness of his comparison with Orpheus.

The six major monuments to Key's memory have been brought forth through great sacrifice of time and effort, not to mention large sums of money, on the part of their originators and supporters. The monuments certainly reflect the nation's indebtedness to Key for "the contribution of this great hymn toward creating that sense of national pride . . . which became at last the inspiration of union preserved and of nationalism established," to quote the words of President Harding spoken at the Orpheus dedication.[31]

Yet the irony in all of this remains that Key himself almost certainly would not have wished to have his name so publicly exalted nor his after-fame blazoned forth in the monumental trappings of markers and statuary. Certainly he was aware of the common longing of men and women to be acclaimed by their fellows while living and long remembered afterward. In one case he might be said to have abetted such a possibility when he consented to have his elegiac sonnet to the memory of the first rector of his church, St.

John's in Georgetown, carved on a white marble tablet and placed alongside of the burial crypt in the church; it is now affixed to the west wall of the sanctuary.

Key's consciousness of the human desire to have one's memory perpetuated is also reflected in the speech he gave in Alexandria, Virginia, in 1814, on the occasion of George Washington's birthday, when he said that he trusted that the great Virginian never felt the chilling thought that his name would be forgotten or disregarded.[32] Yet at the same time Key felt strongly that desire for fame should not be the compelling motive for doing one's duty. His most explicit statement to this effect occurs in his address in Alexandria. In concluding his speech, he declared that whatever of note a person may do in his lifetime—whether toiling long in the public's welfare or risking his life in battle (both of which Key was to do himself)— if he is prompted to this "from the love of power, the dream of ambition, the glory of a name," then he seeks his own aggrandizement— "that it is himself, and neither his country nor his God that he loves and serves."[33]

Indeed, as a devout, practicing Christian, Key believed that one needed constantly to be on guard against the temptation to seek glory on earth or fame among men lest one commit the deadly sin of Pride. Toward the end of his life, in an address at Bristol College, later published as *The Power of Literature*, he cautioned his young audience in these words:

> Still the pride of learning, the love of human applause,
> and the subtle acts of the great adversary of man,
> present powerful temptations, requiring incessant
> watchfulness. It is difficult to be great, and successful,
> and applauded, and humble.[34]

In his own life, Key overcame the difficulties he spoke of by adhering zealously to the Christian creed that admonishes its true followers to practice humility and self denial. For instance, although individuals and crowds applauded him throughout his life for having authored the patriotic hymn, he referred to the song publicly only once. His innate modesty was evident at the inception of the lyric, originally published on 17 September 1814, as a broadside, followed by its appearance in a newspaper on 20 September, both without attribution of authorship.[35] While it is not known whether Key insisted upon anonymity, he did not initiate the publication of the poem. Rather it was his brother-in-law, Judge Joseph H.

Nicholson, who admired the piece so much when Key showed it to him that he immediately sent it to a printer (possibly through the physical agency of John S. Skinner) to be struck off as a handbill. Key's name first appeared as the author on 24 September when the poem, under the lackluster caption "Defence of Fort McHenry," was printed in the *Frederick-Town Herald*.[36] The earliest surviving manuscript in Key's own hand shows that he had not troubled to give the poem a title.[37]

Only four of Key's many poems are known to have been published during his lifetime and two of these are explicitly hymns. In an epitaph for William Hemsley, who died in 1826, initially printed in a posthumous collection of his verses in 1857, Key bespoke his own credo as one who "moved, secluded from the world's vain gaze, / Within a narrow but a glorious sphere / Of Christian duty."[38] Key's own career was conducted in a sphere not quite so restricted as that attributed to his friend in the elegy, but he did constantly strive to avoid the limelight, even though he was active in many causes and supported with his labors and purse numerous private and public good works.

In a letter to his close friend, John Randolph, Key said that a man has no more right to decline public life than to seek it.[39] On this principle he acceded to the behests of Presidents Andrew Jackson and Martin Van Buren to serve as United States Attorney for the District of Columbia from 1833 to 1841. He consciously refrained, however, from seeking elective office. In this connection, toward the end of a speech at a dinner in Frederick in 1834, Key quoted the famous dictum of Andrew Fletcher of Saltoun that "if he could be allowed to make a nation's songs, he cared not who made its laws."[40]

If Key had entertained seriously any hope for immortal fame, which he would have been unlikely to covet because his religion taught that eternal glory could be found only in heaven, it would most likely not have been by means of memorials in bronze and stone. Rather, it would have been through enduring lines of poetry in the spirit of Horace's familiar Ode 30 on literary immortality: *Exegi monumentum aere perennius*—"I have reared a monument more lasting than bronze." The great importance he placed on the creation of a truly memorable poem is indicated by the rhetorical question he addressed to Randolph in a letter of 1813: *"But does it not appear that to produce one transcendently fine epic poem is as much as has ever fallen to the life of one man?"[41]*

Whether "The Star-Spangled Banner" is a transcendently fine poem is not the issue. What is quite certain, however, is that both the poem and the statues that commemorate the writer will be around for a long time to come. As to the writer, one is reminded of the remark made by one of Key's biographers to the effect that he achieved immortality in spite of himself.[42] In like manner, the monuments in California, Maryland, and Washington, D.C., perpetuate his name and fame far beyond any expectation of his own. It is not, moreover, his need that they proclaim; rather, it is that of his admirers down through the years who were impelled to express in engraved bronze and solid stone their reverential homage of the heart.

Notes

1. Delaplaine, *Francis Scott Key*, p. 480.

2. Rev. Brooke, p. 8.

3. Janice Armstrong, "Finances Delay Francis Scott Key Memorial," *The Washington Post*, 28 June 1990. The projected goal of one million dollars was stated in a letter to author from Norman L. Larsen, then president of the Francis Scott Key Park Foundation, Inc., 31 July 1986. This early estimate was soon found to be inadequate but huge donations later from business and industry readily insured that finances would not be an obstacle in completing the memorial. (In November of 1992, the Board of the Foundation changed the official name of the project to "Francis Scott Key Memorial," with the subtitle, "Star-Spangled Banner Monument" [Minutes of the Board of Directors, 4 Nov. 1992, pp. 2-3]).

4. Poster, "Francis Scott Key Park Foundation," enlarged from the Washington, D.C. *Georgetowner*, 12-25 Oct. 1984, in vertical file "Francis Scott Key," Columbia Historical Society of Washington, D.C.

5. Raymond H. Clary, historian, to Gomer Pound, Asst. Dean, Univ. of Miss., Hattiesburg, 8 July 1971, copy received from Diane Palacio, Public Information Officer, Recreation and Park Dept.,City and County of San Francisco on 18 Sept. 1985.

6. "The Celebration," San Francisco *Daily Evening Bulletin*, 5 July 1888, p. 1.

7. San Francisco Recreation and Park Dept., press release, summer 1976, received from Palacio of the Public Information Office of San Francisco City and County 18 Sept. 1985.

8. Clary to Pound.

9. "The Celebration," *Daily Evening Bulletin*, p. 1.

10. Edward S. Delaplaine, "Francis Scott Key ... and his Paradox of Fame," *Potomac Edison Co. Valley of History* (Spring 1967): 3.

11. Ibid.

12. Edward S. Delaplaine, *Doyle and Coppini: Sculptors of the Francis Scott Key Monument* (Frederick, Md.: *Frederick News-Post*, 1987), p. 10.

13. "The Francis Scott Key Memorial," *Munsey's Magazine*, 20, No. 3 (Dec. 1898): 326.

14. Delaplaine, *Doyle and Coppini*, p. 10. The statue of Key was modeled after various portraits of the poet but the one most favored by Coppini was a charcoal drawing by Nellie Thomas, which he felt best captured Key's attitude as one of exultation and inspiration (Edward S. Delaplaine, "The Francis Scott Key Monument, Mount Olivet Cemetery," unpublished and undated typescript, copy furnished to author by Elizabeth B. Delaplaine on 7 June 1994.) The original portrait, given by Thomas to George B. Delaplaine, Jr., now hangs in the corporate headquarters office of The Great Southern and Manufacturing Company, Frederick.

15. Henry Watterson, *The Compromises of Life and Other Lectures and Addresses* (New York: Fox, Duffield and Co., 1903) p. 331. Records of the Mt. Olivet Cemetery in Frederick indicate that a son, Francis Scott Key, Jr. (1806-1866), is also buried in the crypt (J. Ronald Pearson, Superintendent to author, 27 July 1985.)

16. Delaplaine, *Doyle and Coppini,* p. 12.

17. T. J. C. Williams, "Francis Scott Key—the Man," *The Patriotic Marylander*, 1, (Sept. 1914): 28; The Rinehart School of Sculpture, Maryland Institute, 75th Anniversary Catalogue, 1896-1971 (Baltimore, 1971), p. 27.

18. This number included twelve in the flag-of-truce sloop that sailed down the Chesapeake Bay on the mission to rescue Dr. William Beanes from imprisonment by the British: Key, Skinner, Capt. Ferguson and his first mate, with their crew of eight. To these were added, on 8 Sept. 1814, the released Dr. Beanes, plus a temporary guard of British marines, number unknown but not likely to have been more than two or three (Ralph J. Robinson, "The Men with Key," *Baltimore*, 49, No. 11(Sept. 1956): 37, 58.

19. Francis Beirne, *The Amiable Baltimoreans* (New York: E. P. Dutton and Co., Inc., 1941), p. 102.

20. Halt #2—Francis Scott Key Monument, Eutaw Place at Lanvale Street, Baltimore, printed sheet received from Mrs. Robert J. Moore, President U. S. Daughters of 1812, with note of 18 Aug. 1986.

21. Key-Smith, *Francis Scott Key*, pp. 11-12. For further details on the mansion and its environs, as well as a reference to life on the estate during the childhood of the two Key children, see Anne Bertenshaw Cushman, "Francis Scott Key-Patriot,"*The National Republic*, 30, No. 9 (Jan. 1933): 16.

22. Key, *Poems*, pp. 37-39.

23. Delaplaine, *Francis Scott Key*, n. 1, p. 5.

24. The birthdate on the marker is "August 3, 1780," instead of 1 August 1779, which is given in Mrs. Julian C. Lane, *Key and Allied Families* (Macon, Ga.: Press of the J. W. Burke Co., 1931), p. 13, and now generally accepted. The birthdate for Francis Scott Key on the headstone still standing in the family plot at Mt. Olivet Cemetery in Frederick, to which the remains of Key and his wife were transferred in 1866 from the graveyard of St. Paul's Church in Baltimore, reads "August 9th 1780."

25. George C. Mackenzie, Park Historian, *Report on Fort McHenry Statue of Orpheus* (Baltimore: Fort McHenry National Monument and Historic Shrine, 28 Oct. 1959), p. 4 (hereafter *Report on Statue of Orpheus*).

26. Information Sheet headed "Orpheus Timeline," received 28 Dec. 1988 from Scott S. Sheads, Park Ranger, Fort McHenry National Monument and Historic Shrine, National Park Service, U. S. Dept. of the Interior, Baltimore, Md.

27. *Report on Statue of Orpheus*, p. 1.

28. Ibid., pp. 6-7.

29. Information Sheet headed "Who is that Indian?", received from Sheads 28 Dec. 1988.

30. *Report on Statue of Orpheus*, p. 5.

31. Delaplaine, *Francis Scott Key*, p. 479.

32. Ibid., p. 109. For the full text of Key's speech at Alexandria, see Delaplaine, *Francis Scott Key*, pp. 105-115.

33. Ibid., pp. 113-14.

34. Key, *The Power of Literature and Its Connexion with Religion*, p. 11.

35. Filby and Howard, Plate 21, pp. 64-66.

36. Ibid., p. 50.

37. See above, p. xiii.

38. Key, *Poems*, p. 126.

39. Hugh A. Garland, *The Life of John Randolph of Roanoke* (New York: D. Appleton and Co., 1850), II, 106.

40. Delaplaine, *Francis Scott Key*, p. 380.

41. Ibid., pp. 94-95.

42. Weybright, p. 289.

Chapter 7

Endeavors to Commemorate Key in the Nation's Capital

In contrast to several previous efforts to create a major shrine to Francis Scott Key in the national capital, the campaign of the Francis Scott Key Foundation, Inc., established in 1983, required only ten years to do the job. The completion of the Francis Scott Key Park in Washington, D.C., where Key spent most of his adult life, makes it fitting now to tell about earlier endeavors, some successful and some not, to honor Key in his adoptive city. A suitable place to begin would be with the house at 3516 M Street in Georgetown (then an independent municipality), which Key first occupied around 1805, when he moved from Frederick, Maryland, at about the age of 26. For it was at this address that the Keys—"Polly" and "Frank"—reared their eleven children, nine born at the residence. Here, in an adjoining structure to the west, Key had his law office. And he was in residence here when he wrote "The Star-Spangled Banner." When construction of the Chesapeake and Ohio Canal began in 1828, cutting across the back of their beautiful garden that sloped to the Potomac River and threatening to destroy the tranquil ambiance of the stately mansion, Key moved with his family to another house near Third and C Streets.

The M Street house figured prominently in three unsuccessful attempts to create a permanent memorial to Key in the capital. The history of these attempts makes a revealing, if somewhat depressing tale. The movement for the preservation and restoration of the mansion began in 1908, when Francis Scott Key-Smith, a direct descendant of the lawyer-patriot and likewise a prominent District of Columbia attorney, organized the Francis Scott Key Memorial Association to purchase, restore, and preserve the property. At that time the house, except for normal weathering and other deterioration from age, was not too different from when it was occupied by the Key family. Despite the prestige of such founders as Admiral George Dewey of Manila Bay fame and Rear Admiral Winfield Schley, hero of Santiago, the strenuous efforts of the Key Association proved futile and in 1911 the house was returned to private ownership.[1]

A second major effort to restore and preserve the building on the original site was made after 1931, when the United States National Capital Board and Planning Commission purchased the property, but these exertions too failed for lack of financial and political backing.[2] One of the principal movers behind this campaign was the District of Columbia Historical Society, which hoped to establish its headquarters in the building. By this time, Colonel Key-Smith (a World War I veteran, customarily referred to by his military title) opposed the movement. In 1933 he argued against attempts to rebuild the structure, still standing on the site, for now, according to him, "when completed there would not be a floor board upon which Key and his family had ever stepped or a door through which they had ever walked, or a roof under which they had ever slept."[3] What he was referring to was a fact not generally known to the public nor even appreciated by the government officials—namely, that the original mansion had been demolished during the latter part of 1912 and early 1913 and replaced by a structure containing three stores on the ground floor, with storage space above.[4] This was the building which many Washingtonians and visitors to the capital remember to their distaste because of its ugliness and neglect. In April of 1947, a reporter for *The Washington Post* accurately termed it "a dilapidated eyesore."[5] Of the building which tradition had it that Key built for his bride after their wedding in 1802 (but which evidence from the timbers indicated was constructed as early as 1795), only a portion of the original east wall, all of the south wall and the initial foundation remained intact until the razing of the property in 1949. Incidentally, the bricks, stones, and other materials stored in government "bins" around the city in 1947 or after have all been lost or stolen, prompting a quip in the public prints that anyone can lose or misplace a house key but only Uncle Sam could lose Key's house![6]

After World War II, a third and all-out effort was mounted to do something about the Key building. The result was a Congressional measure to:

...construct, furnish, operate, and maintain upon the plot
of ground owned by the United States...in the District
of Columbia, a replica as nearly as may be practicable
of the house in which Francis Scott Key lived from
approximately 1806 to 1828...[7]

Contrary to popular understanding at the time, the act provided
not for the restoration of the house on the original site, but for the
construction of a *replica*, to be located east of the present Francis
Scott Key Bridge on the half-acre now occupied by the Memorial
Park. The cost was estimated by Congress to be $75,000 "or so
much thereof as may be necessary, to carry out the provisions of
section 1 of this act."[8] The bill had the support of virtually every
civic and historical association in Washington and in the state of
Maryland and, what was more essential, the full approval of the
National Commissioners of the District of Columbia. The bill passed
without a dissenting vote in both the Senate and the House.[9]

At the time of the successful Congressional action in mid-1948,
it was already too late to restore the Key residence on its first site
because it stood in the way of a plan for the K Street elevated high-
way. Indeed, by the end of 1947, much of what was left of the original building had already been removed or was in the process, with
timbers, bricks, and other materials stored elsewhere, some under
the Arlington Memorial Bridge.[10] While promotion of and lobbying
for the bill contemplating "restoration" of the house to a new location was going on, Colonel Key-Smith remained publicly silent. He
was, however, familiar with the plan, having been introduced at the
fifty-third anniversary celebration of the Columbia Historical Society by its president, H. Paul Caemmerer, on April 12, 1947.[11] The
principal speaker at that gathering, held at the Mayflower Hotel in
Washington, was Maryland Senator Millard Tydings. Tydings and
Senator Robert A. Taft of Ohio were the original sponsors of the bill
to construct the replica of Key's house. The main purpose of the
April 12 meeting was made clear by Caemmerer, who said, "We
ardently hope that his [Key's] home in Georgetown, properly restored, may become a national shrine."[12] The Society hoped to be
permitted to occupy the restored property as its official quarters.[13]
Nevertheless, Key-Smith presumably did not favor the object of the
measure for reasons analogous to those he had cited during the 1930's
when he had pointed out the "incongruity of a reconstructed and
reproduced house in which Key never lived or ever saw."[14]

But the question of Key-Smith's approval or disapproval of the bill for a replica of the house on a new location became moot on 28 June 1948, when President Harry S. Truman by pocket veto killed the legislation. As reported by *The Washington Post* the following day, Truman acted on the recommendation of the Budget Bureau, which had declared that Key had been "memorialized enough with the erection of the Francis Scott Key Bridge at a cost of $16,000,000 and the provision of Fort McHenry as a national monument in Baltimore, with an annual maintenance cost of between $15,000 and $20,000."[15] Whether President Truman, who in the words of one biographer possessed "an acute sense of history,"[16] agreed with this churlish assessment of the Budget Bureau is uncertain. In any event Dr. F. Regis Noel, attorney and author who succeeded Caemerer as president of the Columbia Historical Society, publicly condemned what he termed "an ignominious pocket veto." This view was expressed over radio station WFMD, Frederick, Maryland, on 8 August 1948. He quoted the President as saying that he "did not like the Bill, or anyone connected with it." By "anyone" Truman probably meant mainly its sponsors, the independent Democrat, Senator Tydings, and the Republican powerhouse of the Senate, Taft. Noel further branded as mistaken the announced figure of $19,000 as the annual cost of maintaining the proposed replica, asserting correctly that the bill "clearly provided an upkeep arrangement which would cost the Government nothing."[17] Another well-known Washingtonian who disagreed vehemently with Truman's Budget Committee's comment that Key "had been memorialized enough" was Carlton J. Corliss, railway historian and an active member of the Columbia Historical Society. In his unpublished paper of 1948, he pointed out that the Key Bridge over the Potomac was neither designed nor built as a memorial to Key.[18] His contention that there was no monument, statue or other memorial to Key in Washington is only partly true.[19] When he wrote this, there was no statue but there were other commemorations.

These memorials in the capital bear either an official or an unofficial cachet. In the former category, if one construes "memorial" in a broad sense, one would include two sets of general issue commemorative stamps: Scott No. 926 (3c,1948) and Scott No.1142 (4c, 1970) and the congressional bill signed by President Hoover on 3 March 1931, making "The Star-Spangled Banner" the official anthem of the United States. Another official recognition of Key appears in the form of a printed inscription on the opaque cover installed in 1982 to protect the original star-spangled banner of 1814, displayed in the center hall of the National Museum of American History, Smithsonian Institution. The seven-line inscription ends with the declaration: "The sight of this flag flying on the morning of the 14th moved Francis Scott Key to write the poem which, in 1931, became our national anthem."

Also involved with U.S. Government sanction is the tablet on the east balustrade of the Francis Scott Key Bridge. This plaque, which was criticized by Corliss as too vague in its attribution to Key, had to be approved by Congress since it was to be attached to government property, namely the bridge built by the Army Corps of Engineers. Such authorization was secured by the National Society United States Daughters of 1812. The dedicatory ceremony was held for the marker on Monday afternoon, 21 April 1924, after the bridge had been in use for fifteen months.[20] Secretary of War John W. Weeks accepted the tablet on behalf of the government.[21] On the morning prior to the bridge ceremony, Weeks made a speech to the Society in which he expressed the gratitude of the nation for the gift. Toward the end of his address he said that one method of keeping in mind the duty of every citizen to contribute to the support and defense of the democracy was "by placing the stirring, patriotic, loyal words of the last verse of the national anthem in enduring bronze where all passersby may read and be continually reminded of the circumstances that may occur again."[22] The original plaque, not so enduring as Weeks imagined, became a casualty when the Potomac span was widened. The new marker, also by the Daughters of 1812, was rededicated on Saturday, 20 April 1957.[23] In September 1993, just prior to the dedication of the park, the plaque was completely refurbished by the Daughters.

Apart from official remembrances, and not counting the holograph Espy copy of "The Star-Spangled Banner"in the library of Georgetown University,[24] three private memorials associated with Key and accessible to the public exist in the capital. The oldest of these by far is the white marble tablet in St. John's Church, a Georgetown Parish, 3240 O Street, N.W. Carved on the tablet is an obituary by Key in the form of a blank verse sonnet on the rector, the Reverend Johannes J. Sayrs, who died in 1809 and was buried beneath the church. Ironically, both the remains of the minister and the tablet placed over them were forgotten for thirty-three years until they were discovered during the excavations for the basement when the church was enlarged in 1843. A new coffin was hastily made and deposited under the new altar. The elegiac stone was brought up and moved to the east wall of the nave. At the installation of a new pulpit in 1967, the tablet was replaced on the west wall. Key's name nowhere appears on the tablet but his authorship was validated in a letter of June 28, 1844, to the parish by the Reverend Sayrs' son, John. In it the son thanked the church for the "delicacy and respect" accorded his father's remains and recalled that the epitaph was "a tribute of affection by his friend F. S. Key."[25] The Latin dedication preceding the verse says simply, "Here lies buried Johannes J. Sayrs, first rector of the Church in which as a servant of Christ, he labored faithfully." The lines in English praise Sayrs for turning his back on earthly ambition and for holding fast to God's love.

Three stained-glass windows in the clerestory of Christ Church, Georgetown, a couple of blocks east of St. John's at 3116 O Street, N.W., constitute one of the more striking evocations of Key in Washington. Services, first held there on Christmas Day, 1818, were attended by him.[26] The present church, constructed on the original site in 1885-86 and consecrated in 1887, had three of its stained-glass windows, given by the Young Ladies Memorial League, in memory of Key. All of the windows, placed in 1887 and honoring former dignitaries of the church, were designed and manufactured by Mayer and Company of Munich, Germany. They are stylistically uniform but because they are not signed, it is not known who the artist was or whether one artist designed them all. Key's name appears at the bottom of the middle window with the words: "In memory of Francis Scott Key Nov. 19th 1817." The date is that of the first organizational meeting of the Founders of Christ Church, which Key was present at.[27] The connection of Key with Christ Church is fairly well known today and visitors occasionally ask about the windows.

At the unveiling of the memorial windows on the Third Sunday in Advent, 1887, the Reverend Albert R. Stuart, in his sermon, referred to the Key windows in these words:

> The name of a more modern poet is there suitably
> inscribed, and henceforth shall the inspired song, which
> celebrates the overthrow of Pharaoh and his host, and
> the deliverance of the children of Israel out of the
> hands of their enemies, remind us of the minstrel

whose immortal lay still fires the heart in this Western
land, and who, as churchman as well as poet, was
present to effect the organization of this church seventy
years ago.[28]

Finally, still another church houses a memorial in the capital to
Key. Like the marker on the Francis Scott Key Bridge, it too is a gift
of the United States Daughters of 1812. It is a brass tablet affixed to
the west wall of the crypt (bookstore section) of Washington Cathedral, Mount St. Albans. The unveiling ceremony took place on 26
April 1931, at a special service conducted by Bishop James E. Free-
man. One of the addresses at this event was given by Colonel Key-
Smith who, according to *The Washington Evening Star*, spoke both
from historical knowledge and family tradition.[29] The tablet itself,
designed by Philip E. Frohman, pictures Fort McHenry against a
rising sun. Above are two American flags in color. One contains
fifteen stars, in a pattern of fives; the other, forty-eight stars for the
number of states in the year of the ceremony. The inscription reads
as follows:

FRANCIS SCOTT KEY

August 9,1780 [should be 1 August 1779]-Jan. 11,1843

And this be our motto—"In God is our trust."
And the star-spangled banner in triumph shall wave,
O'er the land of the free and the home of the brave.

Until 1993, then, none of the existing memorials to Key in the
Federal City were very grand, nowhere near as imposing as the five
great statues erected elsewhere to his memory. The proud boast that
the historian David McCullough made in *American Heritage* magazine about Washington that "No city in the country keeps and com-
memorates history as this one does"[30] seemed not to apply to a hero
of the Republic, whose words in "The Star-Spangled Banner" incar-
nate the national ideals of freedom and valor. Now that the small
but beautiful park stands near a main gateway to the seat of the national government the oft-repeated cries that suitable recognition of
Francis Scott Key in his adoptive city have been both sparse and
tardy will be hushed...but there will inevitably still be some die-
hards who will mutter under their breaths, "Too little and too late!"

Bronze memorial tablet to Key at the Washington Cathedral, Mt. St. Albans, Washington, D.C. Stewart Bros., Gaithersburg, Maryland.

Notes

1. Francis S. Key-Smith, "Obelisk Is Urged at Key Home Site." *The Evening Star*, Washington, D.C., 31 Oct. 1933.

2. Ibid.

3. Ibid.

4. Ibid.

5. "The Fifty-third Anniversary Meeting," *Records of the Columbia Historical Society*, 48-49 (1946-1947): 243.

6. "O, Say, Have You Seen the Now-Missing House of Francis Scott Key?", *People's Weekly* (16 Sept. 1985):56; Tom Zita, "The Case of the Lost Landmark," *The Washington Post*, 13 May 1981, B1.

7. United States, Congressional Record - Senate, 80th Congress, 1st Session, 3 July - 19 July 1947, S.J. Resolution 84, as amended, p. 9031.

8. Ibid.

9. F. Regis Noel, "Recognition of Francis Scott Key in the District of Columbia," radio talk, WFMD, Frederick, Md., 8 Aug. 1948, transcript in vertical file, "Francis Scott Key," Columbia Historical Society of Washington, D.C. (since May 1989 The Historical Society of Washington, D.C.).

10. "O, Say, Have You Seen the Now-Missing House of Francis Scott Key?", p.56.

11. "The Fifty-third Anniversary Meeting," p. 238.

12. Ibid., p. 239.

13. F. Regis Noel, Preservation of the Residence of Francis Scott Key (March 1947), pp. 3-4.

14. Key-Smith, "Obelisk is Urged at Key Home Site."

15. Dorothea Andrews, "President Kills Rebuilding of Francis Scott Key's House," *The Washington Post*, 29 June 1948, p. 48.

16. *Off the Record: The Private Papers of Harry S. Truman*, ed. Robert H. Ferrell (New York: Harper and Row, 1980), p. 2.

17. Noel, "Recognition of Francis Scott Key in the District of Columbia."

18. Carlton J. Corliss, "The Home of Francis Scott Key, Author of Our National Anthem," unpublished paper, circa 1948 (copy donated by Corliss to Columbia Historical Society on 12 Nov. 1953), pp. 2-3.

19. Ibid., p. 1.

20. United States, House of Representatives, 68th Congress, 1st Session, Report No. 53, "Bronze Tablet on the Francis Scott Key Bridge" (17 Jan. 1924).

21. "Key Bridge Tablet Accepted by Weeks," *The Washington Star*, 21 April 1924.

22. Ibid.

23. "Bridge Marker Re-dedicated," *The Washington Star*, 20 April 1957.

24. Copy signed "F.S. Key" and dated at Washington [D.C.] 29 Aug. 1842.

25. Mary Mitchell, *A Short History of St. John's Church Georgetown from 1796 to 1968* [1968], pp. 3, 7.

26. Henry Ridgely Evans, *Old Georgetown on the Potomac* (Washington, D.C., 1933), p. 74

27. Glenn A. Metzdorf, archivist, Christ Church, to author 22 Sept.1988.

28. Albert R. Stuart, rector Christ Church, *A Sermon Delivered in Christ Church, Georgetown, D.C. on the Morning of the Third Sunday in Advent, 1887.*

29. "Daughters of 1812 Unveil Key Tablet," *The Evening Star*, Washington, D.C., 27 April 1931, A-16.

30. David McCullough, "I Love Washington," *American Heritage* (April–May 1986): 27.

Appendix

Francis Scott Key Foundation, Inc.*

Board of Directors

Mr. Steven K. Brisgel

Mr. Robert A. Devaney

Mr. Morgan C. Dodd

Mr. John L. Dreyfuss, *Vice President*

Mrs. Betty Jane Johnson Gerber

Mr. George C. Gerber

Stephen D. Graeff, Esq.

Miss Katherine Murphy Halle

T. Paul Imse, Jr., Esq., *Secretary***

Mrs. Francis Scott Key

Mr. Norman L. Larsen, *First President*

Mr. Richard J. McCooey

Mrs. Jonda McFarlane, *President*

Mr. Thomas G. Pownall

Mr. Mark S. Roberts, *Treasurer*

Mr. Randolph S. Roffman, *Founder*

Miss Caroline L. Scullin

Tony A. Trujilo, Jr., Esq.

Ms. Frankie Welch

---

* From Francis Scott Key Park—The Star-Spangled Banner Monument: Dedication, September 14, 1993.

**T. Paul Imse, Jr., is also the General Counsel

National Advisory Council

The Honorable Dennis DeConcini
The Honorable Robert Dole
The Honorable Daniel P. Moynihan
The Honorable Claiborne Pell
The Honorable William E. Brock
The Honorable Walter E. Fauntroy
The Honorable Robert Keith Gray
The Honorable Lloyd N. Hand
The Honorable Edwin C. Meese III
The Honorable Marion H. Smoak
Mr. Art Buchwald
Mrs. Anna C. Chenault
Mr. Kenneth M. Crosby
Mr. Henry A. Dudley, Sr.
Mrs. Raymond Franklin Fleck
Mrs. Walter Hughey King
Mr. Austin H. Kiplinger
Mr. J. Thomas Malatesta
Monsignor John J. Murphy
Mr. Jeffery S. Parker
Dr. William B. Walsh
Mr. Robert B. Washington, Jr.

Historian Advisory Council

Mr. Gary Browne
Ms. Nancy Miller
Mr. David P. Fogle

Bibliography

Andrews, Dorothea. "President Kills Rebuilding of Francis Scott Key's House." *The Washington Post*, 29 June 1948.

Armstrong, Jenice. "Finances Delay Francis Scott Key Memorial." *The Washington Post*, 28 June 1990.

Arnold, James Riehl. "The Battle of Bladensburg." *Records of the Columbia Historical Society of Washington, D.C.*, 37-38.

Barton, Anna Key. "Recollections of Francis Scott Key." *Modern Culture*, 12 (Nov. 1900).

Beirne, Francis F. *The Amiable Baltimoreans*. New York: E.P. Dutton and Co., 1941.

Braun, Charles. "Let's Waive 'The Star-Spangled Banner.'" *Fact*, 2, No. 1 (Jan.-Feb. 1965).

"Bridge Marker Re-Dedicated." *Washington Star*, 20 April 1957.

Brooke, John T. *A Sketch of the Character of the Late Francis Scott Key*. Cincinnati: Wilson and Drake, 1843.

Browne, C. A. *The Story of Our National Ballads*, Rev. ed. by Willard A. Heaps. New York: Thomas Y. Crowell Co., 1960.

Bryan, W. B. "Diary of Mrs. William Thornton. Capture of Washington by the British." *Records of the Columbia Historical Society of Washington, D.C.*, 19 (1916).

Catton, Bruce and William Catton. *The Bold and Magnificent Dream: America's Founding Years, 1492-1815*. Garden City, Ny.: Doubleday and Co., 1978.

"The Celebration." San Francisco *Daily Evening Bulletin*, 5 July 1888, p. 1.

Clary, Raymond H. Letter to Gomer Pound, 8 July 1971. Public Information Office, Recreation and Park Dept., City and County of San Francisco.

Clephane, Walter C. "The Local Aspects of Slavery in the District of Columbia." *Records of the Columbia Historical Society of Washington, D.C.*, 3 (1900).

Cleveland, Charles Dexter, ed., *Lyra Sacra Americana or Gems from American Sacred Poetry*. New York: Charles Scribner and Co., 1868.

Coles, Henry L. *The War of 1812*. Chicago: University of Chicago Press, 1965.

Conner, Eugene. "William Beanes, M.D. (1749-1829), and 'The Star-Spangled Banner.'" *Journal of the History of Medicine*, 34, No. 2 (1979).

Cordell, Eugene Fauntleroy. *The Medical Annals of Maryland: 1799-1899* Baltimore: The Medical and Chirurgical Faculty of the State of Maryland, 1903.

Corliss, Carlton J. "The Home of Francis Scott Key, Author of Our National Anthem." Unpublished Paper, circa 1948.

Cushman, Anne Bertenshaw "Francis Scott Key—Patriot." *The National Republic*, 30 No. 9 (Jan. 1933).

Delaplaine, Edward S. *Doyle and Coppini: Sculptors of the Francis Scott Key Monument.* Frederick, Md.: *Frederick News-Post,* 1987.

"Francis Scott Key . . . and His Paradox of Fame." Potomac *Edison Co. Valley of History* (Spring 1967).

Francis Scott Key: Life and Times. New York: Biography Press, 1937.

John Philip Sousa and the National Anthem. Frederick, Md.: Great Southern Press, 1983.

Maryland in Law and History. New York: Vantage Press, 1964.

Dozer, Donald M. *Portrait of the Free State: A History of Maryland.* Cambridge, Md.: Tidewater Publishers, 1976.

Evans, Henry Ridgely. *Old Georgetown on the Potomac.* Washington, D.C., 1933.

Ferrell, Robert H., ed. *Off the Record: The Private Papers of Harry S. Truman.* New York: Harper and Row, 1980.

"The Fifty-third Anniversary Meeting." *Records of the Columbia Historical Society of Washington, D.C.,* 48-49 (1946-1947).

Filby, F. W. and Edward G. Howard, comps., *Star Spangled Books: Books, Sheet Music, Newspapers, Manuscripts, and Persons Associated with "The Star-Spangled Banner."* Baltimore: Maryland Historical Society, 1972.

The First Annual Report of the American Society for Colonizing the People of Color . . . and the Proceedings of the Society in the City of Washington on the First Day of January 1818. Washington, D.C.: D. Rapine, 1818.

Francis Scott Key Park Foundation, Inc., Minutes of the Board of Directors, 4 Nov. 1992.

"The Francis Scott Key Memorial." *Munsey's Magazine,* 20, No. 3 (Dec. 1898): 326.

Francis Scott Key Park Foundation, Inc. Fact Sheet.

Francis Scott Key Park Foundation, Inc. *Keynotes.* Washington, D.C.: July 1986.

Garland, Hugh A. *The Life of John Randolph of Roanoke.* 2 vols. New York: D. Appleton and Co., 1850.

The Georgetowner, 1-25 Oct. 1984, Washington, D.C.

[Gleig, George Robert]. *A Subaltern in America: Comprising his Narrative of the Campaign of the British Army, at Baltimore, Washington, &c. &c. During the late War.* Philadelphia: E. L. Carey and A. Hart, 1833.

Halt #2—Francis Scott Key Monument, Eutaw Place at Lanvale Street, Baltimore.

Heitman, Francis B. *Historical Register of Officers of the Continental Army during the Revolution April 1775 to 1783.* Baltimore: Genealogical Publishing Co., 1973.

Hill, Richard. "The Melody of 'The Star-Spangled Banner' in the United States before 1820." In *Essays Honoring Lawrence C. Wroth,* ed. Frederick R. Goff (Portland, Me., 1951).

Hubbell, Jay. *The South in American Literature,* 1607-1900. Durham, N.C.: Duke University Press, 1954.

Jensen, Joseph E. "66 Years Ago This Month . . . William Beanes the Doctor behind 'The Star-Spangled Banner.'" *Maryland State Medical Journal* (Sept. 1980).

"Key Bridge Tablet Accepted by Weeks," *Washington Star,* 21 April 1924.

Key, Francis Scott. *The Power of Literature and its Connexion with Religion.* Bristol College, 1834.

Key-Smith, Francis Scott. "Fort McHenry and the 'Star-Spangled Banner.'" *The Republic Magazine,* 1, No. 4 (April, 1908).

"Francis Scott Key and the National Anthem." Unpublished paper read before the Maryland Historical Society, Baltimore, Md., 14 Oct. 1929 (MD Hist. Soc. MS 2008).

Francis Scott Key: *The Star Spangled Banner: What Else He Was and Who.* Washington, D.C.: Key-Smith and Co., 1911.

"Obelisk is Urged at Key Home Site." *The Evening Star,* Washington, D.C., 31 Oct. 1933.

"The Story of the Star-Spangled Banner." *Current History,* 32 (1930).

Kraske, Robert. *America the Beautiful: Stories of Patriotic Songs.* Champaign, Il.: Garrard Publ. Co., 1972.

Lane, Mrs. Julian C. *Key and Allied Families.* Macon, Ga.: Press of the J. W. Burke Co., 1931.

Lawrence, Edward. "Our National Anthem." *National Magazine,* 14, No. 4 (July, 1901).

Lichtenwanger, William. "The Music of 'The Star-Spangled Banner': From Ludgate Hill to Capitol Hill." *Library of Congress Quarterly Journal,* 34, No. 3 (July, 1977).

Lord, Walter. *The Dawn's Early Light.* New York: W. W. Norton and Co., 1972.

McCullough, David. "I Love Washington." *American Heritage* (April-May, 1986).

Mackenzie, George C. *Report on Fort McHenry Statue of Orpheus.* Baltimore: Fort McHenry National Monument and Historic Shrine, 28 Oct. 1959.

Magruder, Caleb Clark, Jr. "Dr. William Beanes." *Bulletin of the Medical and Chirurgical Faculty of Maryland*, 7, No. 5 (1914-1915).

"Dr. William Beanes, the Incidental Cause of the Authorship of the Star-Spangled Banner." *Records of the Columbia Historical Society of Washington, D.C.*, 22 (1919).

Manakee, Harold R. "Anthem Born in Battle." In Filby and Howard, pp. 29-39.

Manakee, Harold R. and Beta K. *The Star-Spangled Banner: The Story of its Writing by Francis Scott Key at Baltimore, September 13-14, 1814.* Baltimore: The Maryland Historical Society, 1954.

Marbury, William L. "The Seizure and Imprisonment of Dr. Beanes." *The Patriotic Marylander*, 1, No. 1 (Sept., 1914).

Maryland State Archives, Hall of Records, Annapolis, Md., Prince George's County (Wills), Dr. Beanes with codicils, 18 Oct. 1828, pp. 432-37.

Mason, John. Letter to Robert Ross, 2 Sept. 1814. In Svejda, pp. 60-61.

Metzdorf, Glenn A. Letter to author, 22 Sept. 1986.

Muhlenberg, William August, ed. *Church Poetry: Being Portions of Psalms in Verse and Hymns Suited to the Festivals and Feasts, and Various Occasions of the Church.* Philadelphia: P. S. Porter and Co., 1823.

Muller, Joseph, comp. *The Star-Spangled Banner, Words and Music Issued between 1814-1864: An Annotated Bibliographic list with Notices of Different Versions, Texts, Variants, Musical Arrangements, and Notes on Music and Music Publishers in the United States.* New York: G.A. Baker and Co., 1935.

Noel, F. Regis. *Preservation of the Residence of Francis Scott Key.* 2nd prntg. Wilson-Epes Printing Co., March 1947.

"Recognition of Francis Scott Key in the District of Columbia." Radio talk, WFMD, Frederick, Md., 8 Aug. 1948.

"O, Say, Have You Seen the Now-Missing Home of Francis Scott Key?" *People's Weekly*, 16 Sept. 1985.

"Orpheus Timeline." Information Sheet received 28 Dec. 1988, from Scott S. Sheeds, Park Ranger, Fort McHenry National Monument and Historic Shrine, National Park Service, U.S. Department of the Interior. Baltimore, Md.

Poems of the Late Francis Scott Key, Esq., with an Introductory Letter by Chief Justice Taney. Ed. Henry V. D. Johns. New York: Carter and Bros., 1857.

Robinson, Ralph J. "The Birth of the National Anthem." *Baltimore*, 47, No. 2 (Dec., 1953).

"The Men with Key." *Baltimore*, 49, No. 11 (Sept. 1956).

Ross, Robert. Letter to John Mason, 7 Sept. 1814. In Svejda, p. 63.

San Francisco Recreation and Park Dept., City and County of San Francisco, Public Information Office. Press Release, summer, 1976.

Silkett, John T. *Francis Scott Key and the History of the Star-Spangled Banner*. Washington, D.C.: Vintage American Publishing Co., 1978.

Skinner, J. S. "Incidents of the War of 1812." *Maryland Historical Magazine*, 32 (Dec.,1937).

Sonneck, Oscar George Theodore, comp. *Report on "The Star-Spangled Banner" "Hail Columbia" "Yankee Doodle."* Washington, D.C.: GPO, 1909.

Stein, Charles Francis, Jr. *Our National Anthem The Star-Spangled Banner: Its History and Significance*. Baltimore: Wyman Park Federal Savings and Loan Assoc., 1964.

Stuart, Albert R. *A Sermon Delivered in Christ Church, Georgetown, D.C. on the Morning of the Third Sunday in Advent*. 1887.

Svejda, George J. *History of the Star-Spangled Banner from 1814 to the Present*. Washington, D.C.: U.S. Department of the Interior, National Park Service, 1969.

U. S. Cong. Senate. 80th Cong., 1st sess. S. J. Resolution 84, as amended. Washington, D.C.: GPO 3 July - 19 July, 1947.

U. S. Cong. "Full Report," Measure S 2370. Washington, D.C.: GPO.

"The Unveiling of the Original Manuscript of the Star-Spangled Banner." *Maryland Historical Magazine*, 49, No. 4 (Dec. 1954).

Watterson, Henry. *The Compromises of Life and Other Lectures and Addresses*. New York: Fox, Duffield and Co., 1903.

Weybright, Victor. *Spangled Banner: The Story of Francis Scott Key*. New York: Farrar and Rinehart, Inc., 1935.

White, Richard Grant. *National Hymns: How they are Written and how they are not Written*. New York: Rudd and Carleton, 1861.

"Who is that Indian?" Info sheet received 28 Dec., 1988, from Scott Sheads, Park Ranger, Fort McHenry National Monument and Historic Shrine, National Park Service, U.S. Department of the Interior, Baltimore, Md.

Wilberforce, William. *A Practical View of the Prevailing Religious System of Professed Christians in the Higher and Middle Classes, Contrasted with Real Christianity*. 2nd ed. London: T. Codell and W. Davies, 1797.

Williams, T. J. C. "Francis Scott Key—the Man." *The Patriotic Marylander*, 1, No. 1 (Sept. 1914).

Winder, Levin. Letter to Robert Ross, 31 Aug. 1814. In William Marine, *The British Invasion of Maryland, 1812-1815* (Baltimore: Society of the War of 1812), pp. 189-90.

Wroth, Lawrence C. "Francis Scott Key as a Churchman." *Maryland Historical Magazine*, 4, No. 2 (June, 1909).

Zita, Tom. "The Case of the Lost Landmark." *The Washington Post*, 13 May 1981, B1.

Index